The
Witch's
Master
Grimoire

An Encyclopedia of
Charms, Spells, Formulas,
and Magical Rites

The
Witch's
Master
Grimoire

An Encyclopedia of Charms, Spells, Formulas, and Magical Rites

By
Lady Sabrina

NEW PAGE BOOKS
A division of The Career Press, Inc.
Franklin Lakes, NJ

THE WITCH'S MASTER GRIMOIRE
Cover design by Diane Chin
Printed in the U.S.A. by Book-mart Press

To order this title, please call toll-free 1-800-CAREER-1 (NJ and Canada: 201-848-0310) to order using VISA or MasterCard, or for further information on books from Career Press.

The Career Press, Inc., 3 Tice Road, PO Box 687,
Franklin Lakes, NJ 07417
www.newpagebooks.com
www.careerpress.com

Library of Congress Cataloging-in-Publication Data

Sabrina, Lady.
    The witch's master grimoire : an encyclopedia of charms, spells,
formulas, and magical rites / by Lady Sabrina.
        p.   cm.
    Includes bibliographical references and index.
    ISBN 1-56414-482-8 (pbk.)
    1. Witchcraft—Encyclopedias. 2. Ritual—Encyclopedias. 3. Magic—Encyclopedias. I. Title.

BF1566. S25 2000
133.4'3—dc21   00-033911

DEDICATION

Everyone has a special friend—that special someone who is always there to help, give advice, whether you want it or not, and lend a hand when one is needed. I have been blessed with two such special people, two folks who always seem to be there when I need them; to help with computer glitches, and there have been hundreds; to drive me and a sick pet to the animal hospital on New Year's eve; to help with mountains of mail, grocery shopping, and all the things it takes to to run a church and school.

To Autumn and Aristaeus, I thank you, I love you, and I don't know what I would do without you.

CONTENTS

S
179

T
185

U
193

V
196

W

Y

Z

INTRODUCTION

Magick is the most vital force in our lives. It gives us personal mastery over our destiny so we are no longer victims of fate. To study magick is to study life, and to understand the concept of controlled coincidence. Things do not happen randomly, but rather in conjunction or answer to a previously set up condition. The *past* is what controls the *present*, and the *present* is what creates the *future*.

In essence, magick, is the rediscovery of your basic ability to create. What you create or make happen today, is going to reflect on how you are able to deal with tomorrow. If you were to get that much needed pay raise today, you could pay your bills tomorrow, and even plan for something special in the future.

Learning to do magick is like learning to drive—you learn by doing. You take a little time each day to practice, and pretty soon you have it mastered. By learning to drive, you increase your mobility and thus your realm of opportunities. You can suddenly go places and do things you weren't able to do before. Each time you use magick, your ability to control your life increases, and the better your chances are of getting what you want.

Discover how Witchcraft and magick can help you lead a better, more fulfilling life. Arranged alphabetically, the

magickal rites in this book can help you solve those annoying, everyday problems that cause stress and anxiety. Each
entry is fully defined, and then followed by time tested spells
that really work—spells that will fit into your fast-paced life
style. Best of all, you don't need to be a trained initiate, or
have special powers, to make use of the material in this book.
All you need is an open mind, and the desire to succeed.

The word '*Witch*' derives from the Anglo-Saxon *wicca* "a
magickian who weakens the power of evil, or one who is able
to bend reality using natural forces."

Generally, Witchcraft employs the powers of nature to
create a charm, philtre, potion or spell to bring about the
desired change. The physical object then becomes the cata-
lyst or focal point of the magickal operation.

You decide what it is you want, and then you create a
spell or magickal rite to get it. You are in control at all times,
and the outcome depends on your focused will. The only
limitations on magick, are those you place upon it.

Spells are one of the most popular and delightful ways
to approach magick. Since they do not require any specific
amount of room, elaborate equipment, or special training,
anyone can do them. The only thing you really need to make
a spell work is, a strong desire to have something or someone.

So, with all this in mind are you ready to do magick? Are
you ready to cast that magick spell that will help you get the
things you really need and want? If the answer is yes, then
you have the right book in your hand. The charms, spells,
and magickal formulas in this book are easy to follow, and
do not demand impossible-to-find ingredients. In fact, most
of spells and rituals in this book make use of everyday things
like herbs, plants, minerals, and candles. For those magickal
operations that do require special items, such as oils or
incense, recipes are provided.

The only thing you really need to know is "when" is the best time to cast a spell, or how to coordinate your magickal operation to coincide with the phases of the moon. (Moon phases can be found in The Old Farmers Almanac, or on any good Astrological Calendar.) A simple rule of thumb is, use the new moon to begin projects, attract money, or regenerate friendships and health; the full moon to channel energy toward projects involving personal success, career, love, and marriage; the waning moon to get rid of negative influences, and bad situations.

Last but not least, try not to be disillusioned if your magick doesn't work immediately. Some spells just take longer to work than others do. You must have faith, otherwise you block the flow of energy and impede your progress. Remember, every powerful thought you send out leaves an imprint on the etheric world. (For our purposes, etheric pertains to the invisible world, which vibrates at a different level than the physical world. The realm of angels, gods, and other life forms which communicate with humans.) So if you really believe in what you are doing—then it will come true.

Air

Air is symbolically related to breath. It is the subtle realm between the physical and spiritual planes. Air provides us with inspiration, illumination, and the ability to communicate our ideas to others. Air represents new beginnings, the thought process, and creativity. Air helps us to focus and direct energy toward a desired goal. It is our ability to think and reason.

Air Magick

Knot the Wind

Items needed: 3′ strand of blue cord; compass.

The calling or raising of the wind is a very old magickal process, originally used when the wind was vital for sailing. Witches were reputed to harness the power of the wind in a knotted cord, and then sell it to sailors. When untied, the first knot would bring a gentle breeze. The second would bring a strong wind, and the third a gale.

Modern Witches use the knot spell to for inspiration and creativity. To harness the power of the wind you will need a strand of blue cord and a compass. Go to the highest hilltop

Air Correspondence Chart

VALUES	Inspiration, illumination, awareness, perception
COLORS	Blue, silver, white, gray
SYMBOLS	Circle, bird, bell, sylph, flute, chimes, clouds
TOOLS	Wand, rod, staff
PLANTS	Almond, broom, clover, eyebright, lavender, pine
STONES	Amethyst, sapphire, citrine, azurite
PLACES	Sky, mountain tops, tree tops, bluffs, airplanes
ZODIAC	Aquarius, gemini, libra
TIME	Spring, dawn
ARCHANGEL	Raphael
DIRECTION	East
PROCESS	Thinking, reading, speaking, praying, singing

you can find. Face the East. Take several deep, cleansing breaths. Hold the cord above your head. When the wind begins to blow, tie the first knot, as you say the following:

> *I knot the wind*
> *The wind of desire*
> *I knot the wind*
> *The wind that shall inspire.*

Repeat the above conjuration as you tie the second and third knots. Take a few moments to feel the cleansing power of the wind. Ask the wind to free you from all negative thoughts and vibrations. Take your cord and hang it above your desk or work space. Whenever you feel the need for inspiration, untie the first knot and say the following:

I free the wind
The wind of desire
I free the wind
My mind to inspire.

Balloon Magick

Items needed: small balloon filled with helium, parchment paper, 6-8″ string.

Everyone loves balloons. They are like birds, free to float wherever the wind may take them. The idea behind balloon magick is to free your wishes from human bonds so they will have a chance to manifest.

The best time to perform balloon magick is on New Year's Eve. Choose the color of a balloon which most matches your desire, and have it filled with helium:

Red:	Courage, strength, and power.
Green:	Money, luck, and personal goals.
Pink:	Friendship and love.
Blue:	Creativity and peace.
Orange:	Action and attraction.
Black:	Protection and release.
Yellow:	Selling and communication.
White:	Spiritual and psychic awareness.

Ten minutes before the hour of midnight, write your wish on a small piece of parchment paper. With a small piece of string, attach the paper to the balloon. At the strike of midnight let your balloon go as you chant the following passage.

Float now free
Bring to me
What I wish
So Mote It Be!

Turn around and don't look back. Forget about the wish, and allow the powers of the universe to make it come true.

Air Incense and Fragrance

Ambergris (love, lust)

Wear ambergris to attract love. Mix Ambergris with a small amount of vanilla, burn on the night of the full moon to increase passion.

Benzoin (purification, prosperity)

Burn benzoin to clear a room of unwanted vibrations. Mix benzoin with frankincense and burn during the new moon to clear confusion, and increase psychic powers.

Lavender (love, protection)

Wear lavender oil to soothe the mind and body, and bring visions of love. Mix lavender with sage and burn during the waning moon to purify and protect home.

Pine (healing, money)

Burn to clear air and help with breathing problems. Mix pine with eucalyptus and burn to enhance life and bring money.

Sage (wisdom, protection)

Wear sage oil to clear confusion. Place sage leaves under a door mat to protect the home from negativity. Burn sage during the waning moon for protection and to clear confusion.

Star Anise (psychic power, luck)

Burn or wear the seeds to increase psychic power. On a windy day scatter the seeds in the wind to bring luck.

Sweetgrass (spiritual attunement)

Burn sweetgrass to call in the spirits. Mix sweetgrass with lavender and burn to protect the home from unwanted spirits.

AMULET

The amulet is an object that has been left in its virgin state and has been psychically charged with a specific purpose in mind. Amulets are passive in their abilities to communicate energy patterns. Only when their barriers have been crossed do they react or retaliate. For example, the horseshoe that hangs over the door will only bring good luck to those who pass beneath it.

Almost any symbolic object—special stones, shells, wood carvings, statues—can be turned into an amulet. To charge an object as an amulet, hold it in your hand, think about what the object represents, and visualize the object becoming a symbol of that concept as you force your intention into it.

AMULET MAGICK

Ankh

 The ankh symbol stands for everlasting life and regeneration. The ankh amulet works best when made from wood, metal, or faience. The ankh helps its wearer live life to the fullest degree and is sometimes used for success, as well as for protection.

Cross

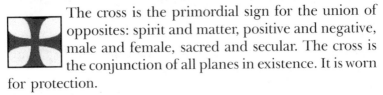

The cross is the primordial sign for the union of opposites: spirit and matter, positive and negative, male and female, sacred and secular. The cross is the conjunction of all planes in existence. It is worn for protection.

Eye or Udjat (the Eye of Horus)

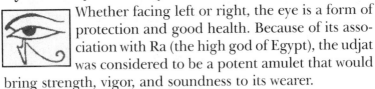

Whether facing left or right, the eye is a form of protection and good health. Because of its association with Ra (the high god of Egypt), the udjat was considered to be a potent amulet that would bring strength, vigor, and soundness to its wearer.

Feather

The feather is a symbol of truth, transcendent knowledge, and power. It represents the wind, the heavens, and the soul's journey to other realms. The feather is considered to be a good omen and brings good fortune and luck in games of skill.

Hecate Wheel

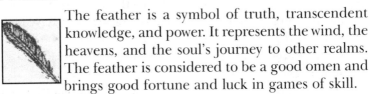

The symbol of the goddess of the crossroads, and emblem of the eternity of Witchcraft. It can be used for protection or to help invoke the goddess herself. The symbol is usually imprinted on a small round disk of silver, wood, or ceramic, and is worn on a cord around the neck or carried in a pouch.

Key

The key is considered to be a universal symbol of life, knowledge, initiation, wisdom, and freedom. The key brings opportunity, offers choice, and signifies new beginnings. A gold key brings good luck, prosperity, and opportunity, and is good for business. The silver key helps one retain knowledge, imparts wisdom, and frees the spirit.

Pentacle

The symbol of the spirit in control of the forces of nature or the elements of ordinary life. This is usually made of silver, gold, pewter or copper, and is worn around the neck for protection from negative vibrations. (This can be consecrated into a talisman, or just worn as a protective amulet).

Scarab

This is a replica of the Egyptian dung beetle. It is usually made from stone or clay. The beetle (scarabaeus sacer) was the symbol of the sun god Khepera, a self created and self-sustaining force. The scarab represents life, regeneration, and renewal—divine providence. To wear the scarab brings health and strength. It also provides powerful protection against all harm.

Unicorn

The unicorn is a lunar emblem of chastity, purity, and divine justice. To own or wear a Unicorn brings security and protection. The root of the Unicorn is a symbol of love, and used to bind the affections of another.

Yin-Yang

 Chinese cosmic symbol. The yin-yang symbol has become very popular with the New Age movement, because it represents the universe and all its possibilities. It is the embodiment and unification of all opposites—the feminine (yin) and masculine (yang) principles. When worn as an amulet it serves as protection and a means to bring one into alignment with the cosmos.

ANIMAL

It has long been believed that humans have a kinship with animals, and that this kinship allows us to draw on their special qualities. When choosing an animal as a totem (a hereditary badge or emblem for a tribe or clan that serves as a personal sacred talisman), you call upon the power of the animal and are drawn into harmony with its strength and power. Totems appear in dreams and bring healing, abundance, strength and power, and protection. Native American Indians believe that when you align your consciousness with that of an animal, that animal will speak to you in a special way, the way of power. This way of power is considered to be very potent. The totem animal then becomes your spiritual ally and safely guides you through life's trials and tribulations. For example, if you feel the need for more independence, you might want to work with the cat. If you are faced with a problem which calls for swift action, then the horse would be a good choice.

The best way to make contact with your power animal is during meditation. Choose a place where you can be alone for at least 15 minutes. Dim the lights and turn off all outside distractions, including the television, radio, and stereo. Seat yourself in a comfortable chair and relax your body. Begin at the top of the head and work downward.

Tilt your head forwards, backwards, and then from side to side, breathing deeply three times each. Relax.

Continue down through the neck, chest, back, arms and abdomen, breathing deeply three times for each body section. Relax.

Then continue on down through the thighs, knees, ankles, feet, and toes. Check all muscles you can feel and be sure that they are relaxed. If your breathing is even and calm, relaxation will come quickly and easily.

As you direct your breathing, exclude all thoughts and sensations and fix your consciousness totally on the breathing process. Let your mind slip into a semiconscious state and ask for your power animal to appear. When the animal comes into focus, relax and allow yourself to connect with the animal on a mental level. Invite the animal to work with you and give you a measure of its power. When you feel you have absorbed the qualities or power needed, thank your power animal, and return to a full conscious state of mind.

Animal Magick

The following animals all have magickal qualities that can be harnessed in times of need. Choose an animal to work with that best represents a personality characteristic you would like to develop or improve.

Bear (introspection, stability, wisdom)

The strength of the bear lies in its ability to enter into a state of hibernation. In this state it is able to digest the year's experience. The bear gains wisdom through sleep in dream time. When warmth and sunlight return, the bear emerges strong, stable, and with renewed vitality. Bear is strongly protective of home and family.

Bear Associations
Direction: North
Element: Earth
Deities: Artemis, Diana, Thor, Cernunnos

The bear will teach you great wisdom. He will also teach you the value of stillness and introspection. When you feel the need for stability, call on the bear during meditation. Ask him to bring you wisdom.

Buffalo (abundance, prayer, thanksgiving)

The buffalo was the major source of food for the Plains Indians. The buffalo provided meat, hide for clothing, and hooves for glue. The buffalo was considered sacred in many traditions because it represented the ideal that when all was in balance there was great abundance. When there was abundance, prayer and thanksgiving were offered in gratitude.

Buffalo Associations
Direction: North and South
Elements: Earth and Fire
Deities: Apis, Cernunnos, Jupiter, Thor, Zeus

When you feel out of synch with those around you or your environment, ask the buffalo for help. Work with the buffalo during meditation. When you feel the need to pray or give thanks for blessings received, ask the buffalo to help you express your emotions in a proper manner.

Cat (independence, secrets)

The cat is very independent, a mighty hunter, and has many secrets. The cat was worshiped by the Egyptians because of its cunning and ability to purge the house of undesirable elements. Bast, the cat-headed goddess, was considered to be a great protector of women. In ancient Rome, the cat was a symbol of freedom. The cat is known for hiding and being secretive.

Cat Associations
Direction: North and South
Elements: Earth and Fire
Deities: Bast, Brighid, Hathor, Isis, Maat, Osiris, Ra

If there is something you need to find out about yourself or others, ask the cat for help during meditation. If you feel overburdened and feel the need for more for independence, invite the cat into your dreams.

Dog (friendship, loyalty)

Dogs have long been considered man's best friend. The dog is loyal to a fault, content with the bare necessities of life, and, like the wolf, protective of home and family. For thousands of years, dogs have been honored for their loyalty. Hermes (Mercury) was frequently accompanied by his faithful dog. Argos, Odysseus's dog, was the only one to recognize him when he returned from the Trojan War. Dogs have a keen sense of smell, hearing, and sight. It is said they can sense evil and death approaching.

Dog Associations
Direction: North
Elements: Earth
Deities: Odin, Lugh, Demeter, Mercury/Hermes, Ishtar

Use the dog when you feel the need for support from your friends, or when you feel loyalties are divided. During meditation ask the dog to protect you from the negative thoughts and vibrations others send your way.

Eagle (spirit, connection to the Divine)

The eagle is believed to be the messenger or connection between humans and the divine. The eagle has the ability to live in the realm of the spirit and yet remain connected to the Earth and its inhabitants. The eagle represents the grace that is achieved through hard work. The eagle teaches humans how to have courage and learn from the lows in life as well as the highs.

Eagle Associations
Direction: East
Element: Air
Deities: Zeus, Indra, Jupiter, Mithras, Apollo

When you need help with spiritual development ask the eagle for help. In meditation merge with the eagle for help with rising above material desires. Ask the eagle to enter your dreams and impart knowledge of about the Ancient Ones.

Elephant (wisdom, stability)

The elephant has always been revered for its size, intelligence, and devotion to family. The Greek philosopher Aristotle admired the elephant for its great wisdom and intelligence. In Hinduism, the elephant-headed god Ganesha is invoked before any undertaking for his wisdom. Ganesha is said to bring stability and abundance to shop owners.

Elephant Associations
Direction: North
Element: Earth
Deities: Ganesh, Indra, Siva

If you're having problems making decisions, work with the elephant for wisdom and stability. If you're considering starting a business or need to attract more customers to your present business, ask the elephant-headed god Ganesha for help.

Horse (swift action, power)

The horse has long been a symbol of swiftness and power. In ancient mythology it is the horse that bears the heroes and the gods across the earth, and even across the sky, at great speed. The horse is physical power and unearthly power. In shamanic practices, the horse enables the shaman to fly through the air to reach the heavens or spirit realm. The horse is able to carry great burdens for long distances with ease.

Horse Associations

Direction: North, East, South, West
Element: Earth, Air, Fire, Water
Deities: Epona, Helios, Brighid,
  Apollo, Godiva, Mars, Artemis

When you need to respond swiftly to a situation, call on the horse. If you need more personal power, or are overburdened by too much work, ask the horse to give you strength.

Owl (clairvoyance, magick, astral projection)

The owl has been called the night eagle because of its connection to the world of spirit. The owl hunts at night. The owl can see in the dark and pinpoint prey by sound. Humans may be afraid of the dark, but night is owl's friend. The owl is silent; you can't hear it when it flies. The owl has often been associated with the Witch because of its connection to the night.

Owl Associations

Direction: East
Element: Air
Deities: Athena, Lilith, Hecate, Bloeuweed,
  Isis, Minerva

During meditation, ask the owl to help you unveil the truth and see things clearly. The owl can also help you learn to interpret omens and intuit dreams. Before doing any kind of divination, ask the owl to be present and help you interpret things correctly.

Skunk (reputation, respect)

The significance of the skunk is no joke. This adorable, furry little animal has a reputation that demands great respect. Due to its distinctive behavior, humans, and other animals, give this tiny, odoriferous creature a wide berth. The fundamental concept here is respect. The skunk's message to all is walk your talk, respect yourself and others, and you will create a position of strength and an honored reputation.

Skunk Associations
Direction: North, East
Element: Earth, Air
Deities: Diana, Cernunnos, Artemis

If you feel a need for respect from friends or family, call on the skunk. He is sure to liven things up. If you live alone, ask the skunk to warn you of danger and protect your home.

Wolf (power, protection, psychic development)

Wolves howl at the moon, they mate openly, and walk silently through the woods. The wolf lives by instinct. The wolf is the pathfinder, the discoverer of new ideas who returns to his family to teach them the ways of the world. The Wolf has keen senses, works with the power of the moon, and is a symbol of psychic energy.

Wolf Associations
Direction: North
Element: Earth
Deities: Loki, Odin, Diana, Artemis,
    Brighid, the Morrigan

When you are in need of more personal power or psychic energy call on the wolf. The wolf will take you to his private den and teach you how to walk silently and work with the power of the moon to build psychic skills.

Astral

The astral plane is the working ground of the magickian, where the truth about all things is revealed. It is the place of angels, demons, and fairies, host to the elemental forces of nature. To the Witch and magickian alike, the astral plane holds the secret of power, the key to the creation of miraculous effects on the physical plane.

The astral plane has often been defined as the realm of visual imagination, a celestial realm where all things are possible. As a result of its ethereal atmosphere, the astral plane remains a great mystery to most. For the fearless explorer, however, the astral plane is nothing more than an uncharted realm waiting to be discovered.

The astral plane is just as real to the astral body as the material plane is to the physical body. To the traveler on the astral plane, the scenery and everything connected with it seems as solid as the most solid material appears to the physical eye. One may travel from one region of the astral to another simply by an act of will without ever moving the physical body.

When consciousness operates outside of the body it takes the mind with it. However, rarely is the mind fully conscious. This is why, although over 90 percent of us project, seldom do we remember our experiences. Usually they are forgotten or passed off as vivid dreams.

Astral Projection

Start by selecting a peaceful place and time of the day where you will not be disturbed. Although this exercise can be done in a chair, it is best to lie flat on your back on a firm, but not hard, surface. Next, stretch out and loosen your clothing. Relax. Follow your breath, fixing your consciousness totally on the breathing process.

Make a conscious effort to go completely limp. Begin with your feet and, working upwards, relax all of the muscles in your body. This should take about four or five minutes.

While in this relaxed state, visualize your inner self becoming light and lifting free of the physical body. Imagine yourself floating directly above the body as though you were on a cloud of air. Allow yourself to experience this feeling for about five minutes and then slowly lower yourself (your astral self) back into your body. Do this exercise several times until you feel comfortable floating and then continue with the next step.

Once you are free of the body, walk into another room. Go slowly and take the time to examine everything in the room. Take note of pictures, how furniture is arranged, and where objects of interest are. Do this exercise several times, and then have someone rearrange the room just prior to your journey. After you have returned to your body, write down exactly what you saw and where everything was positioned. Return to the room and check on your accuracy. The results will then indicate if you actually did astrally project.

ATHAME

The athame is a double-edged knife used to inscribe, or cast, the circle of power onto the earth or floor. It is associated with the element of fire, and it represents strength, power, and the masculine force of nature. Since the athame is a weapon, it also has the power to subdue and banish rebellious entities or spirits.

In magick, the athame is used for directing personal power and to focus energy in a desired direction. The athame also regulates, as well as conducts, the flow of internal expression toward the desired destination during magickal operations.

CONSECRATION OF THE ATHAME

Items needed: Athame; small bowl of water with three pinches of salt added; one white candle; one black candle; sandalwood incense.

On the night of the full moon, place the above items on your altar or small table. Light both of the candles and the incense. Relax and focus on the athame. Pass the athame blade and handle through the flame of the black candle as you say:

All negative thoughts be banished, all unwanted vibrations be gone.

Now pass the athame blade and handle through the flame of the white candle as you say:

Let only the forces and powers I wish be within from this moment on.

Pass the athame through the smoke of the incense, through the white candle flame, and then sprinkle with salt water as you say:

Elements of Air, Fire, Water, and Earth.
To this tool of the magick now give birth.
Blessed and consecrated in this hour
Be thou athame of strength and power.

Wrap the athame in a red silk cloth, and keep in a safe place. Only use the athame for magickal rites and spellcrafting.

Banish

In Witchcraft and magick, banishing usually refers to the casting out of unwanted energies that might influence or impact magickal work. The Witch or magician will usually banish this negative energy from the area he or she will be working in prior to performing any magickal rite or spell.

Banishing Ritual of the Pentagram

Item needed: Athame.

The pentagram is a five-pointed star. It represents the four elements (earth, air, fire, water) subject to the Akasha, or spirit. By all accounts, it is considered to be one of the most powerful protection amulets of the magickal arts. No self respecting Witch or magician would ever leave home without one.

For centuries, ceremonial magicians have used the ritual of the pentagram as a prelude to their mystical rites. The ritual serves to cleanse the working area of negative vibrations. It can also be used to purge oneself of detrimental or obsessive thoughts. The nice thing about the pentagram ritual is that it creates a positive atmosphere for working magic.

Begin the ritual with a short relaxing meditation to help clear your mind and body of stress and dissonant thoughts. When you feel the time is right, stand and face the East. Take your athame in your right hand:

> Touch your forehead and say: *Ateh* (thou art).
>
> Touch your breast and say: *Malkuth* (the kingdom).
>
> Touch the left shoulder and say: *Ve-Gedulah* (and the glory).
>
> Touch the right shoulder and say: *Ve-Geburah* (and the power).
>
> Cross your hands over your breast and say: *Le-Olam* (forever).
>
> Hold the athame up in front and say: *Amen.*

Begin here

This completes the Kabbalistic cross (a ritual devised, in its modern form, by the Hermetic Order of the Golden Dawn), or the opening of the ritual. Take several energizing breaths and continue with the actual inscribing of the pentagrams. Facing East, with your arm outstretched, trace the pentagram with your athame.

When the pentagram is complete, thrust your athame into the center of it, and chant the deity name:

Yod He Vau He.

Proceed to the South. Trace the invoking pentagram in the air with your athame just as you did in the East. When the pentagram is complete, thrust your athame into the center of it and chant the deity name:

Adonai.

Go to the West. Trace the invoking pentagram in the air with your athame. When the pentagram is complete, thrust your athame into the center of it, and chant the deity name:

Eheieh.

Move to the North. Trace the invoking pentagram in the air with your athame. When the pentagram is complete, thrust your athame into the center of it, and chant the deity name:

Agla.

Return to the East, and complete the circle by thrusting your athame into the pentagram you first created. Now step back, and with arms outstretched to form a cross, recite the following with great resolution:

Before me stands Raphael,
Behind me stands Gabriel.
At my right hand stands Michael,
At my left hand stands Auriel.
Before me flames the Pentagram,
Behind me shines the six-rayed star.

Complete the ritual by repeating the Kabbalistic cross as you did in the beginning. The area is now ready for magickal work.

This ritual can be done as a self-protection rite as well. I know some people who do it every morning upon rising. The pentagrams act as a shield of protection throughout the day. The protective power of the rite does fade and dissipate with time, hence the reason it needs to be repeated at regular intervals.

The key to any ceremonial magickal act is visualization. You must be able to project a visual image of the thought-form you are working with, so you can see and feel it. In this case it would be the pentagram, a blazing star of energy and power, an arm's length away.

Besom (Broom)

Hardly anything symbolizes Witchcraft more than the besom (pronounced BEH-sum). The idea of Witches flying on brooms is as old as the Craft itself. We may never find out just where or when this phenomenon began, but it lends certain magick to the tales of old.

The significance of the besom (broom) rests with its ability to sweep, and therefore clean an area of unwanted dirt. European folklore is full of stories about using brooms along with certain incantations while sweeping out the house, the purpose being to sweep out the evil influences along with the dirt. The broom has also been used to form common law marriages. Both parties jump over the broomstick to signify they are joined in a union. Today, many Wiccans and Pagans still jump over the broom at the end of the marriage ceremonies to seal their union.

An authentic besom or Witches broom has seven distinct parts (see illustration).

1. *The Staff Butt*: Usually solid, but may also be hollow and plugged with a wood cork.

2. *The Staff*: The long shaft of the broom, sometimes referred to as the wand, will vary in length, thickness, and texture. Its carvings and decorations also vary.

3. *The Choke Ring*: This binds the upper part of bristles to the staff and is usually made of metal, silver being the best as it represents the moon and goddess. Sometimes there may be several of these used. When more than one is used the first is silver, the second is gold, and the third is copper.

4. *The Stalks (bristles)*: These are grouped evenly around the opposite end of the staff. The stalks should be about half the finished length of the broom.

5. *The Stalk Tips*: The thick ends are held by the choke ring, with the thin ends extending. All of the stalks should be bending in the same direction.

6. *The Splay Ring:* There is only one of these and it keeps the stalks evenly placed about the stalk. This ring is usually made of a very strong pliable cording, as it takes up the strain and pressure of the use that is exerted when sweeping.

7. *The Stalk Butts:* These are the thick ends of the bristles and are bound by the choke ring.

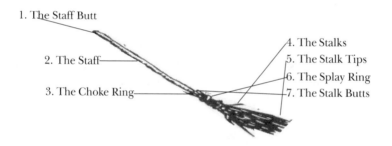

1. The Staff Butt
2. The Staff
3. The Choke Ring
4. The Stalks
5. The Stalk Tips
6. The Splay Ring
7. The Stalk Butts

Besom (Broom) Magick

Besom Blessing

Items needed: a small bowl of salt and one of water, a white candle, a small bunch of fresh rosemary, a censer, a small block of church charcoal, and your besom.

Perform this simple ceremony to bless and consecrate your broom. This will remove all of the negative thoughts and vibrations that may be attached to the broom making it ready for magickal works.

Place the candle, the bowl of salt, and the one of water, along with the censer and rosemary on a small table. Light the charcoal, and the white candle. Sprinkle some salt over the broom and then some water as you say:

Water and Earth
Wash thee clean,
Of all that was
And is unclean.

Place some of the rosemary on the hot coal in the censer. Pick up the broom and pass it through the smoke of the burning herb, and then through the candle flame as you say:

Essence of Air
Flame of Fire,
Cleanse thee of all
But what I desire.

The broom is now ready to use for both mundane and magickal works. Use your broom to purge your house of negative thoughts and vibrations as well as unwanted guests.

Get Rid of Unwanted Guests

Item needed: Besom.

This simple spell works better than anything I have ever found to get folks to leave. We have all had that moment when people have overstayed their welcome and don't have the good sense to get up and leave. Here is a surefire way to get them up and out the door post-haste.

Take a broom into a room that is either facing your unwanted guests or is directly behind them. Close the door. Lay the broom on the floor with the stalk butts facing the direction of the guests. Stand behind the broom, and chant the following:

Get ye out beyond my door
For I'm weary to the core!

Take a few relaxing breaths, and visualize your guests leaving. Put the broom away. Within 10 or 15 minutes they will take their leave, unaware of your magickal nudging.

BINDING

Binding is a powerful spell used in Witchcraft to control the actions of another person, or to render an evil Witch powerless. The binding spell (usually) involves the tying of knots in a cord. This cord is then bound around a picture or effigy of the person in order to control their actions. Binding spells are most often used to stop gossip, or to bind an individual's negative actions so they don't hurt others.

There are some Witches who believe that doing a binding spell is unethical, and goes against the Wiccan Rede. However, many believe in the old adage, "An eye for an eye, and a tooth for a tooth." If you have weighed all the circumstances, exhausted all your resources, and feel justified in your actions, then maybe a binding spell is needed. As with all magick, in the end, it is up to the individual to decide what is right and what is wrong.

BINDING MAGICK

To Stop Gossip

Gossip, no matter who starts it, is always hurtful, and once the damage has been done it is almost impossible to undo. If you feel that someone is gossiping about you, then nip it in the bud before it gets out of hand. I have used the following spell many times with great results. It is not difficult to do, and usually works fairly quickly.

Items needed: One small lamb's tongue, fresh lime juice, three teaspoons of salt, a tag-lock (an object, such as hair, fingernail clippings, photographs, or clothing, taken from the person whose gossip you wish to stop) several yards of red cord or ribbon, plastic wrap, one black candle, a small piece of parchment paper, a red ink pen, and one very sharp knife.

The best time to perform this spell is on a Saturday night during the waning moon. Gather up all the items called for and place them on a small table. Light the black candle. Make a slit in the tongue large enough to put the paper and tag-lock into. On the parchment paper, write the offender's name. Place the parchment paper into the slit in the tongue. Next place the tag-lock into the tongue on top of the parchment paper. On top of the paper, sprinkle the three teaspoons of salt and cover it with the lime juice.

Once the tongue is filled tightly, roll it up in the plastic wrap and wind the red cord around it, chanting the following:

As this tongue doth rot and spoil
Your evil gossip I do foil.
No rest, no peace, nor solace see
Until you stop, so shall it be.

Hang the cord-wrapped tongue in a tree or other high place outdoors for 10 days. At the end of this time take the tongue down and bury it near the offender's home. The gossip will stop.

To Make Someone Hear You

This spell is perfect for making those around you wake up and smell the coffee. When the boss or that special someone turns a deaf ear towards you, this spell will get their attention. You will need a picture of the person whose attention you are trying to get, and a 3'-long piece of white ribbon.

When you are in close proximity to the subject of the spell, focus your attention on the picture. Visualize the person giving you his or her undivided attention. Gaze at the picture, and wind the ribbon around it while you chant:

> *[Insert name] from this day*
> *You hear what I say.*
> *Look now, and see*
> *Look and listen to me.*

Keep the bound picture with you until the person gives you their full attention. Once you have their attention you can unbind the photograph.

To Bind a Lover

This spell is designed to bind the love of one person to another. It works best when both of the parties involved feel the same way about each other.

Items Needed: Two small branches from an elm tree, one piece of red twine, florist's tape, one square of red felt, a photograph of the person to be bound, a small bag of Spanish moss, one red candle.

1. Make a doll by taping the branches together as shown. Fold the red felt square in half and stitch the top, bottom, and side seams together to form the body of the doll. Place the sticks inside the red cloth body as pictured, and fill with Spanish moss. Attach the photograph to the top-neck portion of the doll.

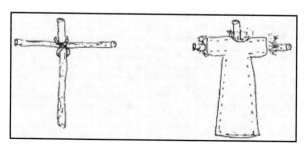

2. Hold the completed doll in your hand and focus your attention on it as you visualize the one you desire. Know that what you do and say to the doll will impact the person it represents.

3. Light the red candle. Pick up the doll and pass it through the flame of the candle as you chant the following:

Lover, lover, come to me
By my side, ever be.

4. Beginning with the head bind the doll with the red twine as you chant the following:

With love I work this magic spell,
That you shall always love me well.
I bind thee tight your passions to inspire,
For I am all you need and desire.

5. Place the doll next to the red candle. Leave the doll and the candle together until the candle has completely burned out. Wrap the doll in red or white silk and keep in a safe place.

BOOK OF SHADOWS

The Book of Shadows, often called a grimoire or black book, is a personal journal in which modern Witches write their invocations, rituals, and spells. Its name comes to us from the distant past when magickal journals were penned in secrecy, beneath the veil of night, and contained mysteries of the shadowy Other World. Because it pages were full of secret formulas, and strange incantations, it was believed that if you possessed a Witch's Book of Shadows, you possessed the key that would unlock the secrets of the universe.

A Witch's Book of Shadows, like any journal, is a collection of personal thoughts and deeds. It will also contain information about drying herbs, observing lunar transitions, and instructions for casting spells to attract love, money, and good health. For the most part, it is an accumulation of magickal practices the writer has found to be useful, and doesn't want to forget.

To most Witches, a Book of Shadows is indispensable. It contains all their magickal recipes. In the same way a cookbook helps create a perfect meal, a Book of Shadows helps create the perfect spell. By keeping a written record of their magickal activities, Witches are able to chart their progress and create a lasting tradition that can be passed on to others.

BOOK BLESSING

It is customary to bless or consecrate your Book of Shadows before you begin to work with it. This is a simple process, and will not require anything other than a candle, pen, and a smudge stick (small bundle of dried herbs held together by cord, usually made of lavender, sage, and sweetgrass).

On the night of the full moon, place the book, pen, candle, and smudge stick on your altar or small table. Light the candle, and speak the following invocation over the book.

By force, by will, by potent power,
The spirits I summon this ritual hour
To charge this book with wisdom well
To cast the perfect rite and spell.

Open the book, and on the first page draw a pentagram with the pen. In the center of the pentagram write your name (or magickal name if you have one).

Close the book and light the smudge. When the smudge begins to burn, pass the book through the cleansing smoke, as you say:

All negative thoughts are banished
All unwanted vibrations are gone
Only the forces and powers I wish
Shall be within from this moment on.

Extinguish the candle and smudge. Wrap your book in black silk and store in a safe place. Although you can share ideas, it is unwise to allow others to read or handle your book. When it comes to Witchcraft, it is best to keep your own counsel.

CANDLE

The history of candle burning is as old as humanity itself. It originates from fire worship. Early man was in awe of fire—it warmed him, protected him, and helped him cook his food. The flame of the hearth was guarded carefully, shielded against the ravages of wind and rain. Over time, fire came to represent strength, power, and the ability to see past the terrors of night.

Symbolically, candlelight represents illumination, the energizing power of the sun, and the spark of life that resides within the human soul. As an agency of the fire element, candles are quick to respond to magickal incantations and creative visualization. The simple lighting of a candle creates an atmosphere of magick, and as the darkness gives way to the light, desires are brought into reality.

Candles can be used by themselves as a form of magick, or they may be incorporated as part of a spell. In either case, the candle itself becomes the point of focus. The color of the candle and its shape and size all play important roles in the art of candle magick. The color signifies intent, the design or shape represents the objective, and the size is equivalent to the amount of time needed to carry out the spell.

Color is of primary importance in candle magick. There are 12 basic colors, which offer different sensory vibrations. Red is the most physically potent and powerful, and violet is the most passive and spiritually receptive. The primary colors of the light spectrum (red, orange, yellow, green, blue, indigo, and violet) emit specific energies, which are symbolic of their intrinsic properties. These colors move energy outward and forward, as well as inward and backward.

In addition to the seven primary colors, there are five additional colors used in the art of candle magick. These are black, white, gray, pink, and brown. Black anchors and absorbs; white encourages and supports; gray is seldom used because it is considered to be void, without movement; pink attracts and entices; and brown stabilizes and sustains.

Burning times (that is, how long the candles should burn) are as essential to candle magick as color is. Each color of the spectrum has its own special wavelength or vibrational frequency. This vibrational frequency is the equivalent of motion and energy, which is the amount of time needed to activate a spell. Therefore, a candle that requires a burning time of four hours will take four times longer to work than a candle that requires only one hour to burn. However, the longer it takes a spell to work, and the more energy involved in its formulation, the more enduring its results.

WORKING WITH CANDLES

The first step in candle magick is to choose a candle whose color and shape represent your desire. Next you will have to dress, or energize, the candle. This is done by anointing the entire candle with an appropriate oil. The oil is usually made from a plant or flower that also represents your desire. Place some of the oil on your fingertips. As you concentrate on your desire, rub the oil onto the candle, starting from the center and rubbing upward. Then rub the oil from

Candle Color Chart

Candle color	Meaning of color	Burning time
Red	Courage, strength, survival, power, lust, immediate action.	One hour
Pink	Love, friendship, open the heart, calm the emotions.	One hour
Orange	Action, attraction, selling, bring about desired results.	Two hours
Yellow	Communication, selling oneself, persuasion, attraction.	Three hours
Green	Love, fertility, money, luck, health, personal goals.	Four hours
Blue	Creativity, tranquility, peace, perception.	Three hours
Indigo	Wisdom, self-awareness, psychic abilities.	Two hours
Violet	Power, ambition, tension, spiritual development.	One hour
Black	Protection, return or release negativity, power.	One hour
Brown	Stability, grounding, earth rites, create indecision.	Four hours
White	Universal color, can be used for any work. All general candle magick.	No set time
Gold	Prosperity, attraction, wealth, increase.	One hour

the center downward. Be sure to cover the entire candle with the oil as you infuse it with your desire.

Candle Magick Hints

→ Whenever possible make your own candles. While the wax is in a liquid form, add a corresponding oil, herbs, or flower petals. For example, if you are doing a money spell you could add Heliotrope oil and mint leaves.

→ When dressing the candle, close your eyes, concentrate, and visualize what the candle represents. See in your mind's eye the manifestation of your desire.

→ Always keep in mind, and allow for, the burning time of the candle when scripting a spell or ritual.

→ When creating your own spells, always use the proper phase of the moon and planetary symbolism. This will align the spell with the natural flow of energy produced by the moon and corresponding planet, giving the spell more power.

Astrological Candle Color Chart		
Aquarius	January 20—February 18	Purple
Pisces	February 19—March 20	Aqua
Aries	March 21—April 19	Pink
Taurus	April 20—May 20	Orange
Gemini	May 21—June 21	Violet
Cancer	June 22—July 22	Green
Leo	July 23—August 22	Red
Virgo	August 23- September 22	Yellow
Libra	September 23—October 22	Blue
Scorpio	October 23—November 21	Gold
Sagittarius	November 22—December 21	Red
Capricorn	December 22—January 19	Brown

Symbolic Image Candle Chart

Candle Shape	Symbolic Purpose
Cat	To change one's luck. Black cat: change luck from bad to good; green cat: good luck with gambling and money; red cat: good luck with love.
Double Action	To attract favorable circumstances and repel negative influences at the same time.
Human Image	Used to represent the individual the spell is being worked on. Red for love and passion; pink for friendship; green for healing and marriage; white for blessing; black for releasing negativity.
Seven Knob	One knob is burned each day to make a wish come true.
The Seven Day	Glass-enclosed novena. Used for specific purpose printed on the candle glass.

CANDLE MAGICK SPELLS

Candle Love-Binding Spell

Use this spell to bind the love of another to you, or to reinforce the qualities of love within an already existing relationship.

Items needed: One red candle, one astrologically colored candle to represent yourself (see chart), and one astrologically colored candle to represent the one you desire, a picture of yourself and a picture of the one you desire, a small jar with a metal lid, love-drawing oil (see page 148), a small sharp knife, and matches.

On the night of the full moon, as close to midnight as possible, place all the items called for on your altar or on a small table. Place the photographs facing each other into the jar and screw the lid on very tightly. Then prepare the astrological candles. Use the knife to write the name of your desired one on his or her candle, and then write your name on your candle. Next dress both candles with the love-drawing oil. Then cut two inches off the bottom of each candle, leaving the wick in tact. Tie the wicks of the two candles together to make one candle, and as you do so say the following:

I tie this knot, to bind the heart
Of my desire [subject's name] to me.

The next step is to attach the tied candles to the top of the jar. Light the red candle, drip a pool of wax on the lid of the jar to act as the adhesive, and then attach the tied candles to it.

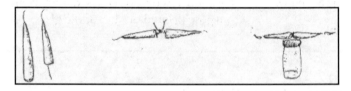

Light the candle that represents you and say the following:

At this time, and from this hour
You feel my love, you feel my power.

Now light the candle that represents the one you desire and say the following:

Feel my passion, feel the fire
I am the one you desire.

When the candles have completely burned out, take the jar and bury it in the ground as close the your loved one's house as possible. Before the next full moon you should be enjoying each other's company.

Love-Drawing Spell

This spell is ideal to get someone to pay attention to you, draw someone you already know closer to you, or make your lover a better lover.

Items needed: A picture of the desired one and some of his or her hair and handwriting to use as tag-locks. You will also need a red cloth pouch, one red image (sexually aligned to the gender you wish to attract), a candle, rose petals, and rose oil.

Place the candle in front of you, along with the picture and all of the needed items. Dress the candle with the rose oil as you visualize your lover coming closer to you and being more attentive. When you feel the time is right, light the candle and chant the following to build power and energy. Direct this energy into the candle.

Candle of power,
From this hour,
Bring unto me
The love that I see.
That he/she shall requite
My attentions this night,
Let him/her see only me.
As I will, So Mote It Be!

Allow the candle to burn completely out. Carry the pouch filled with the rose petals and your lover's items with you whenever you are going to be together. It is also a good idea to wear some of the rose oil.

Money-Drawing Spell

Try this spell the next time you need some quick cash, to pay off that last annoying bill or to buy a gift for a loved one.

Items needed: One green pillar candle, a new one dollar bill, a piece of green construction paper cut into four even squares, and a pen.

On the night of the new moon, place all the required items on your altar, or on a small table. On each square of green paper write out the amount of money you need. Next, write the amount of money you need on one side of the green candle, and write your name on the other side. Wrap the four squares of paper in the dollar bill, making a small flat packet. Set the green candle on top of the packet, and light the candle as you chant the following:

Money, money, come to me,
As I will So Mote It Be!

At the end of four hours snuff out the candle. Repeat the spell every night until the candle has completely burned out. Once the candle has burned out, place one square of the paper, and the dollar bill, in your wallet or purse. Place one square of the paper under your pillow, one square in your desk at work, and the other square under your front door mat. If your request was a reasonable one you should have the amount of money you need by the next new moon.

Black Cat Protection Spell

A good spell to ward off the evil intentions of another, block psychic attack, or turn your luck around.

Items needed: One black cat candle, black cat oil (composed of patchouli and frankincense), and a mirror.

On the night of the waxing moon, as close to midnight as possible, begin the spell. On your altar, or a small table, place the mirror reflecting side up. Dress the black cat candle with the black cat oil. As you do this, visualize your luck changing and good things coming to you. Next, place the cat candle on the mirror and light it as you chant the following:

Black cat power
From this hour
Reflect the light
Make things right.

Allow the black cat candle to burn for one hour. Repeat this spell every night, at the same time, until the full moon. On the night of the full moon, place the mirror with the black cat on it in the moonlight. Repeat the chant, and allow the candle to burn out. When the candle has been consumed, discard any wax left and put the mirror away.

CHARMS

The word charm comes from the French *charme,* meaning chant or song. In magick, to charm is to physically act upon an object or an individual, compelling it to change its course of action. This is usually accomplished through special rhythmic chants, songs, or music which bring the object or individual under the control of the Witch or magician.

To our ancestors, charms were used to control malevolent spirits, which were believed to be the cause of human suffering. The local magician, priest, Witch, or wizard would be called upon by the stricken to utter the right words—speak a spell, formula, or invocation—over the person or property that was under attack. The charm would then ward off the evil eye or malevolent force.

With the advent of the written word, it became popular to imbue charms with a certain amount of permanency by inscribing the magickal verse or formula onto a variety of materials, such a wood, paper, bone, stone, wax, clay, and even precious gemstones and metal. The charm was engraved directly onto the object, and worn or carried by the user.

In contemporary Witchcraft, a charm is a simple poem or verse that is spoken over an object, such as an amulet, to endow it with magickal qualities. The charm, once spoken, exudes a subtle energy, which entices and influences control over its quarry. Once properly charmed, an object is capable of attracting love, creating good fortune, and providing protection for its user.

CHARM MAGICK

Charm of The Yellow Rose

Dab a small amount of your favorite perfume or cologne on a tissue. Take a long-stem yellow rose, and with great feeling and emotion, charm it with the following verse:

The stars above, in darkness shine,
    With light that fills the heavens divine.
So bright with radiance our love glows,
    It out shines the sun, and dims all foes.

Wrap the rose in the scented tissue and place in the refrigerator. As soon as possible, find the opportunity to give it to the one you love.

The Marriage Charm

Bind two small gold rings together with a white ribbon. Hold the bound rings in both hands as you chant the following over them:

With body and spirit
    As these rings entwine
Unite our souls
    Our essence combine.

Place the rings in your pocket or purse. Carry them with you whenever you are with the one you wish to marry.

Charm of Success

Purchase a small gold or brass sun disk pendant from a jewelry or department store. Hang the pendant in your window so that the sun will shine on it ever day. Allow the pendant to absorb the sun's rays for one week. Then on a Sunday morning, stand in the rays of the sun, and, holding your pendant, chant the following charm over it:

Through sun and will, and patient skill,
  Within this disk I now instill,
That I shall fare successfully,
  For this is what I will to be.

Protection Charm

For this you will need a pentagram pendant and a bowl of salt water. Holding the pendant in your left hand and the bowl of salt water in your right, turn to the West. Slowly pour the water over the pendant as you speak the following charm:

Elements of earth and sea
Return to all by power of three.
That which may be sent to me
Unless I have summoned it to be.
I am protected from this night
By the spirits of power and might.

Wear the pentacle for protection on a daily basis. Once a month, at the dark of the moon, repeat the charm to keep your pentacle properly charged.

Personal Power Charm

For this special charm you will need a small diamond or clear cut quartz crystal. On a Sunday morning as close to the full moon as possible, wash your diamond in clear spring water, dry it, and hold it up so the sun's rays shine through it. Focus on the stone and chant the following charm to empower it:

Thou who rule the sun and skies,
By whose power man lives and dies.
Impart thy power, impart thy might,
Within this stone of pure white light.

CRYSTAL

There are many different kinds of crystals, but quartz is the master gemstone of them all. It can be found throughout the world and is especially noted for its healing qualities.

Quartz crystal is composed of silicon and oxygen ($SiO2$) which is considered to be the building block of minerals. In fact, most of our planet is composed of minerals containing $SiO2$. Silicon dioxide is also an important component of the human body, which may be the physical basis for our connection to crystals.

Crystals are formed clear, like ice, they only change color when other minerals are introduced into their structure. The addition of other minerals, such as iron and magnesium, that produces rose quartz, yellow quartz, and amethyst.

The quartz crystal is one of Earth's greatest minerals. It has been used to amplify sound in loudspeakers, microphones, and other audio equipment. In watches and clocks, quartz helps synchronize time. Quartz crystal has also been used in laser and optical technology.

In Witchcraft and magick, quartz crystals are used for good luck charms and protection talismans and as love amulets and healing agents. They are also used in conjunction with various planets and constellations of the zodiac to enhance ritual effectiveness. No matter how they are used, crystals help magnify and extend personal energy and power.

The wonderful thing about working with crystals is that they have the ability to reinforce and sustain human energy vibrations. When this happens, the physical body is strengthened and rejuvenated. This can be very helpful, especially when one is involved in a physically demanding situation.

Quartz crystal is considered to be the master power stone. It is associated with both fire and water. Quartz has the ability to focus the sun's energy rays to ignite wood chips or other combustible material, and it resembles solidified water or ice. Witches wear crystals to represent the Goddess, the moon, and psychic power. Crystals are used for protection, healing, and power.

CRYSTAL MAGICK

Working with crystals is a direct experience with energy as it moves from moment to moment. There is no way to develop standard techniques that can be learned and applied to everyone. People are unique and different, and so are their energy outputs. When working with crystals or stones, the energy output of the individual handling the crystal produces the final outcome.

Learning to work with crystals is easy. Begin by experimenting with a single quartz crystal. Choose one small enough to carry, but large enough to work with. In addition to size, clarity and perfection of the crystal should be considered—make sure your crystal is reasonably clear and free of chips and scratches.

Once you have selected a crystal to work with, you will need to cleanse and charge it. Cleansing the crystal will remove any previous thoughts and vibrations that may be on it. Charging the crystal will program it with your thoughts and vibrations.

Crystal Cleansing

Items needed: Sea salt, an empty bowl, incense burner or smudge pot, charcoal, matches, smudging stick or loose smudge incense, and a protective pouch for carrying the crystal.

Place your crystal in the empty bowl and cover it with salt. Place the bowl where it will receive full sunlight and moonlight for three days. On the fourth day, remove the crystal from the salt and rinse in cool water. Light the smudge stick or smudge incense. Hold the crystal in the smoke emanating from the incense as you chant the following:

All negative thoughts are banished
All unwanted vibrations are gone
Only the forces and powers I wish
Shall be with me from this moment on!

Repeat this process for about a minute or until you are sure the crystal is clean and free of negative vibrations.

Crystal Programming

After a crystal has been properly cleansed it should be programmed for personal use. This is a simple process which imbeds personal feelings and desires deep within the heart of the crystal. Once programmed, a crystal becomes a unique magickal tool attuned to its owner's individual vibratory frequency.

Programming a crystal for personal use is easily done. Crystals attract and hold energy vibrations, which makes them useful tools for focusing and directing energy. Think of your crystal as a mini-computer, and what you program into it designates what it will be able to do. The thought-forms used to energize the crystal will determine the power and frequency level at which it will vibrate. If you program the crystal with love, it will radiate love. Conversely, if you program the crystal with determination, aggressiveness, and force, these will be the vibrations it will emit.

Once a crystal has been cleaned, it is ready to be programmed for personal use. Of the many ways to program a crystal, the following two methods are the most common.

Hold the crystal in your hand and create a thought-form (mental picture) of what you want to happen. For example, if you want to program the crystal for good health, visualize yourself energetic and in glowing health. You will then need to force this vision or thought-form into the crystal. To intensify the visualization, chant or speak your desire directly into the crystal.

The other way to program a crystal involves holding the crystal over your heart. Create a thought-form of your desire and allow this picture to flow directly from your heart into the crystal. To empower the mental picture, reaffirm it audibly through prayer or chant.

Crystal Gazing

At the stroke of midnight, just before the moon begins to wax, is the best time to look into the future. You will need a crystal, a clear glass bowl filled with spring water, and a white taper candle.

Place your crystal in the bowl and cover it with the spring water. Place the candle just behind the bowl and light it. With your right index finger, slowly stir the water around the crystal as you chant:

Blessed spirits of the night
Bless me now with second sight.

With your intense focus, the water will begin to cloud over, and a mist of psychic awareness will fill the bowl as you stir the water. When the mist begins to flow out of the bowl, stop stirring the water and look directly into the bowl. Focus your attention on the crystal and repeat the following:

Fire and water, crystal clear
Let the visions now appear.

Visions of the future will appear. When the visions begin
to fade, make a mental note of what you saw. Snuff out the
candle and place your crystal under your pillow. The crystal
will provide you with more information during your dream
time. Later, write your visions down in your book of shadows.

Dragon

The dragon is a fantastic beast that appears in almost every mythological tradition throughout the world. Often depicted as a mix of several different creatures, it represents the four elements of life: air, fire, water, and earth. The dragon has the wings of a bird and is covered with the scales of a fish or snake. It is capable of breathing fire, and usually guards a horde of treasure deep within the earth. In pre-Christian Europe and the Far East, the dragon was seen a symbol of power, virility, and superhuman strength, and was considered to be a friend of mankind.

In magick, the dragon is wholly beneficent and is seen as the manifestation of life-giving waters (the serpent), and the breath of life (the bird). Generally it is considered to be a celestial power, and has the attributes of both the sun and moon, masculine and feminine, good and evil sides of nature. The dragon and serpent are usually interchangeable as representations of the unmanifest and the creation of form and matter.

The dragon represents the highest spiritual power, the supernatural, and the spirit of change. When you align your forces with those of the dragon, you gain strength and power. Its magick can help you overcome negative thoughts and it can teach you how to live abundantly.

DRAGON MAGICK

Dragon Prosperity Spell

This spell is designed to create prosperity. It works best if you have a job and are looking for a pay raise or bonus.

Items needed: One large green pillar candle, dragon's blood incense, incense burner and charcoal, dragon prosperity oil, a green silk pouch, five new coins (a penny, nickel, dime, quarter, and half-dollar), and an altar or small table.

(*To make dragon's blood incense*, mix 1/2 tsp. dragon's blood resin with 1/2 tsp. allspice, 1/2 tsp myrrh resin, 1/2 tsp. dried orange peel, 1/2 tsp. sandalwood powder. To the mixture add 3-drops cinnamon oil, and 3 drops orange spice oil. To make dragon prosperity oil, mix 5 drops cinnamon oil with 3 drops orange spice oil and 2 drops sandalwood oil in a small bottle.)

(*To make dragon prosperity oil*, in a small bottle mix 5 drops cinnamon oil with 3 drops orange spice oil, and 2 drops sandalwood oil.)

The first thing you will need to do is engrave the figure of a dragon on the candle. This can be easily done using a ball point pen or small sculpting tool. The engraving does not have to be an elaborate work of art, just a simple outline will do.

Begin on the night of the new moon. Place the dragon candle on your altar with the incense burner in front of it. Place the coins on the left side of the candle and the silk pouch on the right side.

Light the green candle and charcoal. When the coal is glowing red, sprinkle some incense on it. Pick up the penny, hold it tightly, close your eyes and visualize the dragon in his cave. See his treasure and all the wealth he guards. In your mind's eye, slowly approach the dragon. Show the dragon your coin. Then, with great respect, ask the dragon to expand your wealth as you say:

O great dragon of wealth and power,
I greet thee in this sacred hour.
Great good fortune on me now shower.
That my prosperity shall blossom and flower.

Stay with the dragon for a short time. Listen to what he says, and take heed of his advice. When the dragon begins to fade, leave his cave and return to the present. Place the penny in the green silk pouch. Thank the dragon by saying:

I thank thee great dragon of power and might
For granting my wishes on this night.

Leave the candle to burn for four hours and then snuff it out. Repeat this spell every night until all of the coins have been placed in the green pouch. When the last coin has been placed in the pouch, allow the candle to completely burn out. The rite is then complete.

DRAWING DOWN THE MOON

It was believed by the ancient Greeks and Romans that Witches had the power to draw down the moon from the sky. This assumption is not without reason. Should a witch be seen invoking the Goddess beneath a full moon, she would naturally be standing in a position where the beams from the moon would highlight her person, making it seem as if she had a direct link to the lunar orb.

In modern Wicca, the rite of Drawing Down the Moon or Calling Down the Moon is of considerable importance. During this potent invocation, the practitioner enters a trance-like state of altered consciousness and draws the essence of the Goddess into herself. The energy of the Goddess is then focused toward a magickal act, divining the future, or spiritual revelation.

Drawing Down the Moon involves being completely open and receptive to the feminine spirit of nature. It is usually done out of doors, beneath a full moon. Stand with your arms outstretched, pointing upward at the moon. Once you are relaxed, focus on the moon. Feel its rays reach down and touch you. When you feel the time is right, slowly begin the following invocation, building to an emotional climax.

INVOCATION FOR DRAWING DOWN THE MOON

Bewitching goddess of the crossroads
Whose secrets are kept in the night,
You are half remembered, half forgotten
And are found in the shadows of night.

From the misty hidden caverns
In ancient magick days,
Comes the truth once forbidden
Of thy heavenly veiled ways.

Cloaked in velvet darkness
A dancer in the flames
You who are called Diana, Hecate,
And many other names.

I call upon your wisdom
And beseech thee from this time,
To enter my expectant soul
That our essence shall combine.

I beckon thee O ancient one
From far and distant shore,
Come, come be with me now
This I ask, and nothing more.

EARTH

Earth is physical reality. It symbolically represents both the womb and the grave. Earth is the element that brings forth life and then reclaims it. Magically, earth is viewed as the final outcome, a place where the other elements can physically manifest their nature. Earth is our base of operation, in which we exhibit the final product of our imagination. Earth is the magician's altar, a place to create change in accordance with will.

EARTH MAGICK

Ivy Love Spell

Use this spell to win the affections of the one you desire if he or she has not returned your feelings of love.

In an earthenware pot, plant a fresh cutting of ivy (which represents constant and ever growing love). Braid two lengths of red and green ribbon together. Wind the ribbon around the pot and tie in a large bow. Place the potted plant in a window where it will receive sunlight during the day and moonlight at night.

Earth Correspondence Chart

VALUES	Responsibility, perseverance, experience, authority.
COLORS	Yellow, brown, russet.
SYMBOLS	Square, cornucopia, spindle, scythe, salt.
TOOLS	Shield, pentacle, flail, horn.
PLANTS	Alfalfa, cotton, oats, patchouli, vetivert, wheat.
STONES	Moss agate, jasper, malachite, peridot, tourmaline.
PLACES	Caves, forests, fields, gardens, canyons.
ZODIAC	Capricorn, Taurus, Virgo.
ARCHANGEL	Auriel.
TIME	Midnight, winter.
DIRECTION	North.
PROCESS	Responsible, practical, organized, steady, grounded.

Each time you water the plant, chant the following:

As the ivy does grow
To my true love show.
I shall be his (her) delight
Both day and night.

Be sure to nurture the plant carefully, for as it grows, so will you gain the love of the one you desire.

The Love Box

For this spell, you will need a small ceramic or wooden box and the following items:

- ↣ A scoop of earth from your desired one's front yard.

- ↣ A lock of your desired one's hair.

- ↣ Seven pine needles (for constancy).

- ↣ One rosebud (for love).

- ↣ A lock of your hair.

- ↣ A pinch of fresh lavender (for harmony).

Place all the items into the box. Close the box and bind it tightly with red and gold ribbon. At midnight on the night of the full moon, bury the box beneath an apple tree. Draw a heart in the earth above the spot where the box is buried. Chant the following nine times:

Power of earth
To love give birth.

When you have completed the spell, turn and walk away. Do not look back. The love you desire will certainly come your way.

Earth Prosperity Spell

This spell is very effective if you are looking for a job. Begin on the night of the new moon. In a small brown paper bag, collect earth from the following places:

- ↣ A bank near where you live.

- ↣ A store where you enjoy shopping.

- ↣ The company you would like to work for.

- ↣ The nearest crossroads.

- ↣ Railroad tracks running North and South.

The following night, inscribe an orange candle with the name of the company you would like to work for. Place the candle in the center of your altar (or on a small table). Around the candle, make a small circle with the earth you have collected, as you verbally declare all the things you will do once you have the job.

 Light the candle. In your mind's eye see yourself working at a job, spending money, shopping at your favorite store, making decisions, and even traveling. Allow the candle to burn for two hours. Repeat each night until the candle has been consumed. Scoop up the earth that surrounds the candle and place it in a small orange pouch, along with a small crystal. Carry the pouch with you when looking for the job you desire.

EARTH INCENSE AND FRAGRANCE

The following herbs, oils, and incense mixtures should be used when doing earth magick. Because herbs are related to earth, their vibrations will enhance all your magickal works, especially those affiliated with the earth element.

Honeysuckle (money, protection)

Wear honeysuckle oil to attract money. Mix honeysuckle oil with a bit of vervain for protection. Burn honeysuckle incense on the night of the new moon to attract money.

Magnolia (fidelity)

Wear magnolia oil to keep loved ones faithful. Burn magnolia incense in the bedroom to maintain a faithful relationship.

Patchouli (money, lust)

Wear patchouli oil to entice passion in the one you love or desire.

Vervain (protection, purification, youth)

Mix vervain and patchouli oil together and wear as a veil of powerful protection. Mix vervain with sage to cleanse and protect your home from negative influences. A drop of vervain oil on a cloth placed inside your bed pillow will keep you feeling young.

Vetivert (love, luck, money)

Wear a drop of vetivert to attract both love and money. Gamblers rub vetivert oil on their hands before playing cards for good luck.

EYE

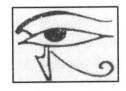

The eye is considered to be the primary organ of sense perception. It is closely associated with light, the spirit, and the sun. The eye symbolizes spiritual and mental perception and is considered to be the mirror of the soul, the organ of spiritual and mental expression.

The right eye is associated with activity, the future, and the sun. The left eye is associated with passivity, the past, and the moon. In some cultures and religions (such as Buddhism), a third eye is envisioned in the middle of the forehead, just above the nose, and is considered to be a symbol of inner vision and power.

In magick, heterotopic eyes are those that have been transferred anatomically to various parts of the body, such as the hands, wings, torso, arms, and different parts of the head. These eyes are the equivalent of spiritual sight or clairvoyance. When the eyes are situated on the hand, it signifies that the individual has great clairvoyant powers.

E ❖

The most widely used eye symbol in magick is that of Horus. In ancient Egypt, the right eye of Horus, the sky god, was his solar eye, and the left eye was his *udjat eye*, or eye of the moon. The *udjat eye* symbolizes the power of light and was one of the most sacred and powerful protective amulets in Egyptian magic.

Depending on its employment, and surrounding symbolism, the single eye can represent the forces of good or evil as the single eye of god, or the destructive power of the Cyclops.

Fairy

Fairies are magickal creatures endowed with the powers of shapeshifting and invisibility. They dwell in an invisible kingdom known as middle or lower earth. Often depicted as small humanoid beings with diaphanous wings, they look like tiny angels. However, they are not angels, they are unpredictable, and they can be as puckish as they are benevolent.

Sometimes referred to as "little people," fairies are an important part of most cultures, religious traditions, and folk beliefs throughout the world. In European culture, they are believed to be nature spirits who dwell in the trees, plants, and waterways. Christianity seems to think they are Lucifer's fallen angels and therefore evil. Other folk beliefs, especially those of African origin, view them as souls of the dead or ancestors.

Celtic culture has probably done the most to promote the idea of fairies, who are believed to be the descendants of the small, dark, Neolithic people who invaded early Europe. Being small and dark and living close to the land allowed them to quickly hide from their enemies. This ability, along with their elusive mannerisms, led people to believe they were capable of magick, shapeshifting, and invisibility.

When the old Pagan religions died out, the fairies were relegated to the realm of myth and fantasy. We find the Great Goddess transformed into the Good Fairy Godmother or Queen of Fairies. The Horned God became the Fairy King, Puck, and the trickster. Those with less appealing traits were relegated to the realms of devils and demons.

The Fairy Realm

Auki

The mountain spirit of Peru who inhabits the high Andes, called upon by the brujos (shamans) to heal the sick. The brujos will call the auki by whistling. The auki will descend, and channel its power through the brujos.

Bogie

A frightening goblin of English folklore. The bogie is described as little, black, and hairy. It is considered dangerous, mischievous, sly, and is renowned for its intelligence. Parents would use the threat of the bogie to frighten young children into good behavior.

Brownie

A household spirit popular in northern English and Scottish folklore, the brownie is a very small, brown, shaggy human and usually dresses in ragged brown clothes. Brownies are considered to be most industrious when it comes to such household chores as grinding grain, churning butter, and plowing. They love to help humans with their work, especially with tedious tasks. Brownies are thanked with a bowl of fresh cream and freshly baked bread. If criticized, they will undo what they have already done and destroy a good deal more.

Deva

In New Age philosophy, devas are the guardians of nature and are responsible for building up forms on the inner planes as well as on the physical plane. The devas hold the keys of fate for all forms around us. They appear in every shape and size, from the earthly gnome to the highest archangel.

Elf

Found in British, Scandinavian, and Teutonic folklore, elves are tiny, human-shaped supernatural beings who resemble little old men. However, elf maidens are considered to be young and very beautiful. They live in communities or kingdoms, hidden in the hollows of trees, long burrows, or in mounds. They are ruled over by an elf king and queen. Elves exert their powers over humans whenever they can, usually with mischievous intent. When offended by humans they will take revenge by stealing babies, cattle, milk, and jewels, and they have been know to enchant the offender and hold them for years. Elves emerge after sunset to dance in the moonlight, swim in shallow pools, and frolic in the woods.

Gnome

Considered to be a nature spirit or elemental, gnomes resemble dwarfs with small stocky bodies, and usually appear as little old men dressed in monks' habits. Gnomes live in the earth, the element they represent, and are the guardians of mother nature's treasures.

Goblin

A grotesque, diminutive, malicious earth spirit. Popular in European folklore, goblins are said to be knee high, with heavy gray hair and beards. They inhabit the homes of humans, where they indulge in poltergeist activities. They are not fond of adults but do seem to like children, as they have been known to protect them and bring them gifts.

Imp/Impa

A mischievous minor fiend often described as being a child-like offspring of the Devil. Imps manifest in many different forms. The most popular form is that of an evil-looking infant with tiny horns protruding from its head and tiny wings from its shoulders. Imps were the star attractions at Witch trials, as they were considered to be the familiars of the accused.

Leprechaun

The folklore of Ireland is filled with famous tales of this fairy shoemaker. The Leprechaun is depicted as having a wizened face, gray beard, and twinkling eyes. He wears a red jacket with silver buttons, brown breeches, black, silver-buckled shoes, and a high crowned green hat. In pictures, he usually appears in an apron, holding a hammer and mending shoes. This wee creature is tricky, and likes to make mischief with humans. He also has a reputation for having a huge stash of gold hidden in a secret place.

Nymph

Nymphs are female water spirits that appear in classical Greek and Roman mythology. They are portrayed as beautiful your maidens dressed in gossamer gowns, with long flowing hair. The nymphs would attend to gods and entertain them with dancing and music. Like most spirit creatures, nymphs were both benevolent and malevolent toward humans.

Pixie

These small creatures are said to have red hair, small, turned up noses, pointed ears, and pale, youthful faces. They especially attracted to gardens in bloom, and take up residence under toadstools. Pixies have mixed emotions when it comes to humans. However, if they take a liking to someone they will help him or her out with household chores and gardening. They also like to work with gold, silver, and bronze. Some believe that the residue from their metal work is the main ingredient in Pixie dust, a magickal powder use to make wishes come true.

Fairy Magick

Because fairies are connected to nature, their spells are usually performed outdoors. A small brook, a secret lily pond, the base of your favorite tree, or a field of wild flowers all make excellent settings for fairy magick. Even large, lush window boxes, overflowing with fragrant herbs and delicate blossoms, can serve as a haven for the wee folk.

Fairy Wishing Spell

For this spell you will need a small white birthday candle, a silver coin, seven moon cookies (sugar cookies cut into crescent moons), and a secluded wooded area where you can be alone.

As you walk through the woods, keep a close eye out for Fairy circles, small circular areas surrounded by inedible red fungi with white spots. It is believed that fairies meet within these rings to celebrate their magickal rites. When you find a fairy circle, carefully place your coin in the center of it. Set the candle on top of the coin, light it, and make your wish. When the candle has completely burned out, place the moon cookies around the coin, state your wish aloud, and then walk away. If you return to the spot and your coin and candle are gone, you will know that your wish has been granted.

Fairy Enchantments

If there is one thing that a fairy takes great pride in, it is the ability to charm and enchant an unsuspecting human.

Using herbs, flowers, and mystical incantations, the skillful fairy makes a magickal dust that can be used to inspire love, protect loved ones, and bring forth great riches when sprinkled on the ground or over an unsuspecting human.

Fairy Dust

Items needed: A blender or coffee grinder, silver glitter, dark blue jar, three silver coins, silver paint or a silver marker, and the following dried herbs ground into a fine powder:

+ 1 tbsp. woodruff
+ 1 tbsp. clover
+ 1 tbsp. rose petals
+ 1 tbsp. jasmine
+ 1 Tbsp. meadowsweet

Place the powder into the dark blue jar. On the outside of the jar, inscribe the following symbol with the silver paint or marker:

On May eve as the sun begins to set, place your jar of Fairy dust in the center of a Fairy circle. Kneel next to the circle, uncap the jar, and chant the following nine times:

Nature spirits and fairy friends
Bless this dust to serve my ends.
I place my trust and faith in thee
To bring me love, wealth, and prosperity.

Rise and leave the area for one hour, giving the fairies time to bless your powder. When you return, thank the fairies for their help, retrieve the jar, and leave the three silver coins in its place.

Sprinkle the powder over a sleeping loved one to increase passion, sprinkle on the threshold of a business to attract new customers, or sprinkle around the perimeter of your home to invite happiness and good will.

Fairy Garden Money Spell

Gardens, especially ones designed with a purpose, will attract good fairies, gnomes, and all manner of beneficial creatures. Cultivate a nine foot circular patch of earth. Around the perimeter, place small stones and crystals.

In the center of the circle place a stone garden gnome. Around the gnome, plant a mixture of marigolds and clover. Each day, spend some time with the gnome. Make friends with him and beseech him to make your wealth grow as the garden does. To ensure he follows your wishes, chant the following each time you water the garden.

> *Nature spirits everywhere*
> *My love and energy I now share.*
> *With cool water this charge I give*
> *Plants now grow, blossom, and live,*
> *Your gift of wealth I seek to share*
> *In return I give you loving care.*

As the garden grows, so will your wealth and prosperity.

FIRE

In the practice of magick, the element of fire relates to the South, the realm of energy and power. The potential of this element is expressed in the crackling flames of fire, lustful passions, or disciplines requiring strenuous endeavor.

The element of fire promotes transformation and purification. Fire is the life-giving generative power of the sun. From fire we receive inspiration and personal power. It is the force that motivates and drives all living organisms. It represents personal willpower and the force that sparks creation.

Fire Correspondence Chart	
VALUES	Energy, transformation, strength, power, courage
COLORS	Red, red-orange (as in flames), amber
SYMBOLS	Triangle, lightning, flame, salamander
TOOLS	Sword, dagger, fire pot, double-headed ax
PLANTS	Basil, bloodroot, dragon's blood, ginger, orange, tobacco
STONES	Ruby, garnet, diamond, bloodstone, flint, sunstone
PLACES	Volcanoes, ovens, fireplaces, deserts
ZODIAC	Aries, Leo, Sagittarius
ARCHANGEL	Michael
TIMES	Summer, Noon
DIRECTION	South
PROCESSES	Passion, anger, impetuous, progressive, valor

Fire Magick

Fireplace Magick

This simple spell is used to make a wish come true, and is especially effective if done on New Year's Eve. It is also great way to end a romantic evening or group gathering.

Items needed: One square of red paper and piece of yellow paper ribbon for each person doing the spell, a small bottle of heliotrope oil, and a jar of basil.

Light a fire in the fireplace. Write out your wish on the square of red paper. In the center of the square, place a drop of the heliotrope oil and a pinch of basil. Fold the paper into a packet and secure with the yellow ribbon.

Gaze into the fire. Visualize what you want. Speak your wish out loud, and then toss the packet into the fire. As the fire consumes the packet, chant the following:

Blazing fire, burning bright
Make my wish come true this night.

Friendship Spell

This spell is done to create friendship or make a friendship stronger. You will need a red candle to represent yourself and a pink candle to represent your friend.

On the night of the full moon, write your name on the red candle and your friend's name on the pink candle. Place the candles opposite each other on a table, about one foot apart.

Light your candle, light your friend's candle, and chant the following:

As the candle flame doth flicker and glow
So this friendship shall blossom and grow.

In your mind's eye, visualize you and your friend together, sharing warm moments and having a good time. When the vision begins to fade, snuff out the candles. Repeat each night until the next full moon. At this time, allow the candles to burn out. The spell is ended and your friendship should be going strong.

FIRE INCENSE AND FRAGRANCE

Allspice (money, luck)

Wear allspice oil to increase luck, especially when gambling. Allspice is added to incense to attract money.

Basil (love, wealth, protection)

Add basil to food, or sprinkle around the house to attract love. Carry basil in a pouch to attract money and wealth. Make a wreath of basil tied with red and black ribbon for protection.

Carnation (strength, healing)

Wear carnation oil to promote physical strength. Add carnation oil to frankincense resin and burn to promote healing.

Frankincense (spirituality)

Burn Frankincense to consecrate ritual space. Anoint candles to be used on the altar for ritual with frankincense oil.

Galangal (money, lust, protection, psychic power)

Powdered galangal is sprinkled on the ground to bring good luck and money. Pieces of galangal are carried to attract money. Galangal is burned as an incense to increase psychic powers. The powder is sprinkled under the bed to promote lustful feelings.

Heliotrope (wishes, money, healing)

Wear heliotrope oil to attract money. Burn heliotrope incense to attract money and make wishes come true.

Orange (divination, love, luck, prosperity)

Mix dried orange peel, rose petals, and lavender buds to make a love drawing sachet. Anoint forehead with orange oil before doing divination. Mix orange and allspice oil together and wear for good luck.

Rosemary (love, lust, healing, protection)

Burn rosemary and Lavender for protection and healing. Place a sprig of rosemary under your loved one's pillow so he or she will dream of you. Anoint green candles with rosemary oil to attract love and lust.

GLYPH

In Witchcraft and magick, glyph is a term used to describe a powerful symbol that represents a person, place, or thing. When the glyph is consecrated, and/or acted upon, it can ward off psychic attack, illness, and bad luck. Most glyphs are a combination of an individual's name and birth date. These are inscribed upon a piece of parchment with special ink and corresponding astrological symbols. The glyph is n worn for protection by the person for whom it was made.

PERSONAL PROTECTION GLYPH

To make the protection glyph, you will first need to work out your name numerically. Use the chart below to change the letters in your name into numbers.

Letter-Number Correspondence Chart

1	2	3	4	5	6	7	8	9
A	B	C	D	E	F	G	H	I
J	K	L	M	N	O	P	Q	R
S	T	U	V	W	X	Y	Z	

Example: **S a n d y   L a n e**
           1 1 5 4 7   3 1 5 5

Add numbers together = **32**
Add numbers together to get a single digit: **3+2=5**

To make the glyph, you will need a small round metal disk, a black marking pen, and a pouch to place the disk in when you are finished. On one side of the disk, write the single digit for your name. On the other side, inscribe this symbol:

As you draw the symbol, visualize a protective shield surrounding you, protecting you from the negative thoughts of others. Seal the disk by inscribing a pentagram in the center of the symbol. Place the disk in the pouch and carry for protection.

GOLEM

Most magicians are familiar with the legend of the Golem, a figure made of clay and wood that was brought to life through a process discovered by Rabbi Yehuda Low. According to Kabbalah, Jewish mysticism, the formula for creating a Golem was found in the *Sefer Yetsirah*, a theory of creation

BNLS CHIX BRST V	1 @ 9.16	9.16	F
GROUND BEEF CHUC	1 @ 7.85	7.85	F
BEEF FLORENTINES	1 @ 15.10	15.10	F
CK HEARTY WH	1 @ 2/4.00	2.00	F
SHRF COFFEE	1 @ 2.39	2.39	F

SUBTOTAL	5	36.50
TAX		0.00
TOTAL		36.50
		36.50
		40.00
		3.50

THANK YOU
FOR YOUR
BUSINESS

11/9/2004   JON D   6:55:40 PM

69571

69185

9
16
13
―――
38

1
38

28
――――――
6+6 = 12 = 3

WELCOME TO
ANETOS
(605) 742-9721

THANK YOU
FOR YOUR
BUSINESS

derived from the first 10 numbers and 22 letters of the Hebrew alphabet.

In the original rendition, the prophet Jeremiah and his son Ben Sirah create a Golem in the image of a human being. The word emeth (truth) is then carved into its forehead, bringing the Golem to life. Later stories have the Golem being brought to life by a piece of sacred parchment on which the name of God has been inscribed.

The size, shape, and characteristics of a Golem are determined by the individual making it. It is believed that organic material, such as clay, wood, and bone, produce the best results. Once assembled, the Golem is ready to be animated through a process called ritual sculpting, which usually takes place in a properly consecrated ritual space.

Using a single candle of pure beeswax and a sanctum regnum incense (made from frankincense, myrrh, and gum arabic), the Golem is presented at each of the four quadrants as the archangels are evoked. During this time, special incantations are performed to infuse the Golem with the will and intention of the magician. As the ritual concludes, the candle is extinguished, and the magician will then spend several hours visualizing the Golem coming to life, forcing energy into it. The entire process can take days, even weeks, to accomplish.

Once the process has been completed, the psyche of the Golem should be fully animated and ready to do the magician's bidding. At first the Golem will be given simple tasks to do, such as protecting the magician's personal belongings. In time, as the Golem grows and develops, so do its chores. Rewards come in the form of praise, gifts, and the psychic energy that is offered by the magician.

The Golem is an extension of the magician's will and power, very much like an etheric double. Should the magician need assistance during a magickal operation, the Golem is there to lend a helping hand. The Golem may sound like the answer to hired help, but beware: Like most magickal undertakings, there is another side of the coin to consider. Once it has been brought to life, the Golem and its creator are psychically bound together, and as time passes it becomes increasingly difficult (if not impossible) for one to exist without the other.

GYPSY

Gypsy is a corruption of the word Egyptian and refers to Little Egypt, or lesser Egypt. The people who came from this area on the outskirts of Egypt were highly skilled in natural magick and were especially gifted in their ability to divine the future. A cast of turbulent wanderers, the Gypsies traveled through Europe during the Middle Ages.

By the early 16th century, the Gypsies had spread across Europe. They were extremely clannish, and did not marry or socialize outside of their blood line. They lived, traveled, and worked in family groups called cumpanias.

The Gypsies were vagabonds, traveling in ornate horse-drawn wagons or caravans know as vardos. Living off the land, the Gypsies subsisted off their magickal and divinatory talents. Famous for their powerful love potions, protection charms, and psychic abilities, the Gypsies were often the targets of Christian persecution. Even though the Gypsies all but disappeared, their legacy of magick survived. Today, through historical and magickal text, it is possible to learn about the Gypsies' way of life, and legendary magickal ways.

GYPSY MAGICK

Gypsy Love-Drawing Oil

When the moon turns new, pick a wild rose and sprig of fresh rosemary. Put the rose and rosemary into a bottle filled with rose oil and tightly cap. Around the neck of the bottle, tie a green satin ribbon.

On the night of the full moon, in a place where you can be alone, hold the bottle so the rays of the moon will shine directly upon it and chant the following nine times:

Mother of the moon, mother of love,
Descend to me from far above.
With your power this spell I fashion
Infuse this scent with lustful passion.

Anoint your shoulders, breasts, and wrists with the oil. When your intended is exposed to the scent, he or she will not be able to resist you.

Gypsy Love Potion

According to Gypsy lore, this is guaranteed to make the one you desire fall head over heels in love with you. To make the potion you will need one ripe apple, several rose petals, and a sweet red wine.

In a white porcelain bowl, crush the apple and rose petals until they are pulp. Drain the juice into a glass or bottle. Fill a glass with the wine and add the apple-rose mixture to it. Stir the mixture with the third finger of your left hand three times. As you do this, speak the words of love you feel into the mixture.

Next, take a new wine glass and inscribe the following symbol on the bottom of it:

Pour the mixture into the wine glass and serve to the one you desire. When your desired one drinks the wine, he or she will fall immediately under your spell.

Gypsy Gold Attraction Pouch

The Gypsies were very fond of ornate pouches and would endow their contents with great powers. To attract business, the Gypsy would add magickal items to his or her money pouch. When the pouch was blessed, it became a powerful attraction magnet.

On a Friday night as the moon begins to wax, collect the following items:

- ✦ One gold coin.
- ✦ Three small acorns.
- ✦ One ounce gold dust.
- ✦ Three pebbles from a crossroads.
- ✦ One small magnet.
- ✦ One high john root.
- ✦ One ounce marigold petals.

Place the items you collected in a gold silk pouch. Then, on a piece of parchment paper inscribe the following sigil:

Put the sigil into the pouch along with the other items. Hold the pouch in your right hand and speak the following blessing over it:

Money from here and money from there
To meet my needs with plenty to spare
Treasures that bring security and calm
Gold and green now fill my palm.

Hang the pouch from the mirror in your car or carry in your purse or briefcase. Once a month, re-bless the pouch with the words above so it will continue to work for you.

Gypsy Protection Spell

The Gypsies placed great value in the power of cards. This simple spell was used to protect the family from those wishing them harm. On the face side of the ace of spades, the person's name is written in red ink. On top of this, place a black candle and three black crow feathers.

At midnight, before the moon turns new, light the black candle and chant the following:

Let there be no delusion,
You are bound by confusion.
I now send you on your way,
Far from me you shall stay.

When the candle has burned out, bind the card with red and black thread. Take to the nearest crossroads and bury. The intention is to cause confusion in the victim's life so he or she will no longer be a bother to you.

Spell for Wisdom and Truth

This spell will help you find the happiness that comes from wisdom and truth. On the first Sunday after the new moon, inscribe a small circle in the earth. In the center of the circle draw the following symbol:

Place a small gold candle on top of the symbol and arrange nine apple seeds evenly around it in a circle. Light the candle and say the following.

Let now wisdom and truth be my guide.
Follow me and bless me all the days of my life.

When the candle has burned out, place the apple seeds in a small pouch and wear around your neck. Truth and wisdom will follow.

Hair

Hair represents strength and energy. Early Christians shaved their heads to show their devotion to the religion. In some cultures, it is seen as an act of purity to have all body hair removed before marriage. In the Middle Ages, cutting a person's hair had symbolic value judicially and was done to dishonor the law breaker.

In cultures where magick was practiced, a person's shorn hair could signify the actual person and could be used accordingly. Even hair color was considered. In the Middle Ages, blonde hair was considered good or heavenly, and red hair was a sign of evil or Witchcraft.

Modern practitioners of Witchcraft still use hair to link a person to a spell. It is believed that if you have a person's hair, you have a part of them and that what you do with or to the hair will then affect the person directly. Hair is often used in healing rituals and binding spells.

Hair Magick

Braid That Binds

This spell is intended to bind you to the one you love. You will need three long strands of hair (about 12 inches) from your head and from your loved one's head, a strip of red ribbon, and a small cherry wood box. Braid the strands of hair together as you chant:

Let thy thoughts be only of me,
None other shall you ever see.
By braid I bind thee forever,
That I shall lose thee never.
Thou art bound in wake and sleep,
Mine forever thou heart to keep.

Tie the braid off with the red ribbon. Place the braid in the cherry wood box and keep next to your bed.

Protection Spell

For this protection spell you will need a lock your own hair, a small white envelope, sealing wax, and a seal with your initial on it.

Place all the items on your altar or on a small table. Light the candle, put the lock of hair in the envelope, close, and seal with the wax and your initial.

Chant the following over the envelope, and then put it in a safe place.

Sealed within I shall be
That no harm will come to me.

Herbs

Herbs provide us with an abundance of medicinal, as well as magickal substances. Most herbs are easily grown and cared for, because in reality they are weeds. Herbs will grow in the shade, in between rocks, thrive in sandy soil, and can go for long periods of time without water. Once planted, herbs return year after year and serve as a useful as well as decorative ground cover.

Along with their physical and medicinal qualities, herbs are filled with natural energy and power. Through ritual, Witches will focus and direct this energy toward a desired goal. Once magickally charged, the herb will then actively attract or repel incoming vibrations as designated. Because of their life force and energy, plants make wonderful psychic conductors, as well as powerful talismans.

The Urban Herb Garden

The Window Box

Even the city apartment dweller has room for herbs. Take clutter off the kitchen windowsill and replace it with an attractive planter, filled  with fresh, growing herbs. The following herbs and small plants are attractive and easy to grow, and are the staples of most love spells.

Window Box for Love and Attraction				
Basil	Violets	Parsley	Rose	Tarragon
Cardamom	Thyme	Rosemary	Yarrow	Lemon balm
Dill	Endive	Daisy	Dulse	Bleeding heart.

The Patio, Balcony, or Porch Planter

Terra cotta strawberry pots are ideal for the urban gardener. When they are grouped together in varying sizes, they make an attractive addition to any balcony or porch. The main portion of the planter, located in the center, is usually filled with tall and bushy herbs, and the side pockets usually hold small or trailing plants. The following herbs and plants thrive in strawberry pots and make welcome additions to attraction and prosperity spells.

Window Box for Attraction and Posterity				
Marigolds	Marjoram	Green bean	Goldenrod	Dill
Fenugreek	Woodruff	Tomatoes	Irish moss	Poppy
Alfalfa	Cinquefoil	Clover	Mint	

HERB MAGICK

Herb Protection Pouch

Use this spell to protect your property or a loved one you may feel is in danger.

Items needed. One black candle, one small stone from a cemetery, black cloth pouch filled with a pinch of each of the following herbs and plants:

✦ Vervain

✦ Wormwood

✦ Thyme

✦ Oak bark

✦ Spanish moss

On the night of the dark moon go into the woods, and find a place where four paths cross (crossroads). Stand in the middle of the cross point of the path, visualize what it is you want to protect, and then chant the following nine times:

Power of herb, power of wood,
Power of stone, power of good,
Power of earth, power of tree,
From all this evil now be free.

When you have finished with the chant, dig a small hole and place the pouch in it, and cover with earth. Place the black candle on top of the spot where you buried the pouch. Light the candle and repeat the chant nine more times. Extinguish the candle. Leave the pouch where it is for three days. At the end of that time return and retrieve the pouch. Carry the pouch for protection or give it to someone in need.

Herb Love Spell

This spell will give your new romance a kick-start. As the plant grows, so will the love and affection between you and the one you desire.

Items needed: One small basil plant, earth, one rose quartz crystal, and a red flower pot.

Write your name and the name of the one you desire on the front of the pot. Just before the moon turns full, put the rose quartz in the bottom of the pot, fill the pot with earth, and plant the basil in it. As you do this, chant the following:

By earth and stone and Mother Earth
To love and passion now give birth.

Repeat the chant each time you water the plant. As the plant grows and thrives, so will your lover's affection for you.

All-Purpose Healing Amulet

Items Needed: Green cloth pouch, red cloth paint or marker, and a pinch of each of the following herbs:

* ✦ Garlic
* ✦ Eucalyptus
* ✦ Cinnamon
* ✦ Sage

Lay the pouch on a hard surface and smooth out all the wrinkles. Using the red cloth paint or marker, draw the following "healing symbol" on the pouch.

When the paint is dry, fill the pouch with the herbs. Hold the pouch and visualize good health. Carry the pouch with you during the day, and at night place it under your pillow. Use the pouch until the affliction goes away.

HEX

The term hex comes from Early American Folk belief, and implies the use of magick to hurt or harm another person's body, family, or property. The hex was usually cast by a hex-doctor or sorcerer, who used deep concentration and symbolic imaginary to affect his or her target. Although the hex is considered to be an evil curse or black magick, the process of hexing can be used in a positive manner to bring about good luck, heal the sick, and conjure up good fortune.

A good example of using the hex process to bring about favorable results still thrives in this country. The Pennsylvania Dutch have been using a form of hex-craft for centuries to protect their property, heal the sick, and maintain a measure of personal peace and harmony. To the modern city dweller, Pennsylvania Dutch hex-craft may seem a bit odd. But to early Germanic people, magick was tantamount to survival. The early pioneers of this country did not have it easy. If they did not maintain a strict vigilance over loved ones and make the best of what Mother Nature had to offer, they never would have endured.

The most noticeable aspects of the Pennsylvania Dutch magickal system are the elaborate symbols, or hex signs, that they use to decorate their barns, homes, and village stores. These colorful signs represent hundreds of years of tradition and come in many patterns and sizes. Similar to a Voodoo veves, hex signs are combinations of natural symbols that convey specific intentions. They are used to protect property, attract love, bring good fortune, and enlist the aid of the four elements for agricultural purposes.

The annual cycle protected by the circle and the eight-rayed star, symbol of life and balance.

The sign of strength and courage. The double eagle denotes watchfulness and the tulips represent fertility.

How To Make A Hex Sign

Be sure you have all the tools you will need to complete the sign you have designed or found. If you are doing an original drawing, plan it out first on a blank piece of paper. Be sure that the picture will represent the result you desire. On a round disk of wood or metal, draw out the hex sign. As you draw, ask a blessing. For example: "This is the universe that surrounds me. It is blessed with the universal power of the almighty forces of creation."

After the initial drawing is completed, paint the sign with colors selected for their symbolic harmony with the aims of the sign. For example, a design featuring a rooster, representing watchfulness and spiritual vigilance, might be painted red and white for power and protection.

Once the hex sign has been painted, it should be blessed and consecrated to the purpose for which it was made. This is done by holding your hands over the sign and charging it with personal energy and power. If the hex sign is for protection, you will want to recite a simple chant or prayer that will convey your thoughts verbally as you focus on the sign. For example: if the hex sign was made for protection, you might want to say:

Powers of the present and the past
There is none beside thee.
Be now a guard, remain steadfast
In perfect love and purity.

As soon as the sign has been blessed, you will want to hang it outside of the house in a place for all to see. If the sign is for protection, you might want to place it over or next to a bedroom window. If the sign is for love, hang it over the kitchen door or window. If the sign is for prosperity, fertility, and good fortune, hang it over the front entrance of your home.

Ice

Given that water is symbolic of potential, swift movement, and the ability to nurture, it only stands to reason that ice be given symbolic jurisdiction as well. Water flows, promotes growth, responds to our needs, and is one of the four elements required for survival. With magick, water is used to attract love, encourage healing, and advance transition. Ice, on the other hand represents the stultification of development and impedes progress. Magickally ice is used to slow things down, impede, or otherwise stop forward motion.

Ice Magick

A Spell to Freeze Your Enemy

Use this spell to stop or impede an adversary or irritating person who will not take no for an answer.

Items needed: One small opaque container, a bottle of Tabasco sauce, and a picture of or handwriting from the person you want to stop.

Place the picture or handwriting in the bottom of the container. Sprinkle some of the Tabasco sauce over it and then fill the container with water. As you place the container in the freezer, say the following with great emphasis:

Fiery hot, and then frozen cold,
Your powers are now put on hold.

Sand and Ice Love Spell

If you feel the one you love is not responding as he or she should, use this spell to get things going. You will need a flat container of finely grained sand (please do not use cat litter). Several hours before you plan to perform this spell, freeze a fresh red rose in a container filled with water.

Begin this spell by writing your lover's name in the sand and then draw the following symbols around it:

Take the iced rose and place it in the center of the sand, so that it covers your lover's name. As the ice melts, so will your lover's heart. Keep the rose next to your bed as a symbol of eternal love.

INCENSE

Incense, like music, speaks without words to the conscious mind. It stirs the emotions as it brings back memories of things, events, places, and people long since forgotten. Because of its evocative nature, incense has always played an important role in both religion and magick.

Priests and magicians have long believed that the burning of incense will attract higher spiritual forces. It is believed that incense has the ability to deliver directly to the realm of the gods those prayers and wishes spoken into its smoke. These prayers are then blessed and their petitioners' wishes granted.

Essentially, incense can be made from any substance as long as it smells good when burned. Some of the more traditional ingredients used are clove, cinnamon, sandalwood, and resins like frankincense and myrrh. The reason these aromatic substances smell so good is that their essential oils are released when they are heated, emitting a perfumed

Allspice Berries *(spicy)*	Use for money, luck, and healing.
Bay Leaves *(mellow)*	Use for protection and purification.
Cassia Bark *(cinnamon like)*	Use for love, protection, psychic power.
Cloves *(warm-spicy)*	Use for love, protection, and money.
Deer's Tongue Leaves *(sweet-woodsy)*	Use for lust and psychic power.
Eucalyptus *(like camphor)*	Use for healing and protection.
Lavender Flowers *(flowery)*	Use for love, protection, and happiness.
Myrtle Leaves *(like eucalyptus)*	Use for love, fertility, and money.
Orris Root *(violet like)*	Use for love, lust, and attraction.
Patchouli Leaves *(musky)*	Use for love, money, and fertility.
Rosemary *(heady-medicinal)*	Use for love, lust ,and protection.
Sandalwood *(rich-mysterious)*	Use for protection, wishes, and spirituality.
Star Anise *(spicy)*	Use for psychic power and luck.
Tonka Beans *(like vanilla)*	Use for love, luck, and attraction.

smoke. The fragrant oils contained in the following herbs, spices, and woods make them a source of natural incense that can be burned alone or in combination with other substances.

Generally, incense comes in two forms: combustible, which is in the form of cones, sticks, and blocks, and non-combustible, which in the form of powder or resin. The simplest kind of incense to make is the noncombustible kind, as it does not require mucilage or an ignitable substance. Also, noncombustible incense is far less messy and frustrating to deal with.

The base for noncombustible incense is generally talcum powder and/or sawdust and/or powdered spice. Saltpeter is added to make the incense burn. A powerful essential oil is then added for fragrance along with a dye for color. The incense is then burned in a censer on small church charcoal blocks.

To create your own magickal incenses, begin with a base (talcum, sawdust, or a special spice blend). To the base, add the appropriate herbs or resins. Grind the mixture into a powder, and then add a few drops of perfume or essential oil. Mix well to blend oil and powder together. Place the incense in a jar with a tightly fitting lid and then label accordingly.

The following formulas are for noncombustible incense. You will need a grinder, a small mixing bowl, an eye dropper, measuring spoons, and jars with lids. Grind all of the herbal ingredients into a fine powder, add the oil and mix thoroughly. Store in glass jars or plastic bags.

Try to time your incense making with the appropriate moon cycle. For love and attraction use the new to full moon, for personal or psychic power use the full moon, and for protection or banishing use the waning moon.

Before you begin to make any magickal substance, take a few moments to think about what you are doing and why. As you blend the ingredients together, firmly instill your intent into the mixture. Visualize your desire, audibly chant or speak this desire as you work, forcing it into the very essence of the incense. This extra effort of focused energy will enhance the incense, and the magickal work it is intended for.

MAGICKAL INCENSE RECIPES

Love-Drawing Incense

1 part sandalwood base
1 part lavender buds
1/2 tsp. basil
1/2 part orris root powder
3 drops rose oil
1 drop lavender oil

* color red or pink

Money-Drawing Incense

2 parts talcum base
1 part cassia chips
1 part crushed allspice
1 part frankincense
1 part marigold petals
3 drops frankincense oil
2 drops clove oil

* color green

Protection Incense

2 parts talcum base
2 parts patchouli
2 parts sandalwood
3 drops patchouli oil
3 drops sandalwood oil
3 drops sage oil

* color black

Full Moon Incense

2 parts orris root powder
2 parts lavender buds
2 parts myrrh powder
2 parts calamus
3 drops jasmine oil
3 drops rose oil
3 drops gardenia oil

*Color comes from powdered paint

JEWELS

Magickally, jewels and gems are associated with spiritual truths due to their innate talismanic attributes. Like all natural substances, gemstones contain an energy or life force of their own. The color, shape, and size of the stone are what determine its magickal value. For example, because of its red color and association with fire and the planet Mars, the ruby projects energy, strength, and power. Therefore, it would make a wonderful talisman to lift the spirits of someone with low self-esteem.

PROPERTIES OF JEWELS AND GEM STONES

Amber: Not exactly a gem stone, but still highly prized among Witches and magicians. Amber is a fossilized resin that was favored among the ancients for its rich, golden, honey color. Amber represents the congealed rays of the setting sun and is worn for strength, protection, beauty, and love.

Amethyst: A vibrant purple quartz, considered to be very spiritual in nature. Amethyst has been valued for thousands of years as an instrument of magick. It will help clear confusion, aid in prophetic dreams, and protect against self-deception.

With no negative qualities, amethyst is very calming and spiritually uplifting.

Aquamarine: Sometimes called "sea water," it belongs to the goddess of the ocean. It is a pale blue-green color and is carried to enhance psychic power. The stone is also used for healing, purification, and to bring love and happiness.

Carnelian: A warm, red-orange in color, smooth to the touch. The stone is carried for courage and to curb jealousy and envy. It is also believed that the carnelian will prevent certain skin diseases which has made it popular with healer. Carnelian can also be used for courage and sexual energy.

Crystal Quartz: Considered to be a master stone of power. It is associated with both fire (because of its ability to focus the sun's rays to ignite combustible material), and with water (because it looks like ice). Witches wear crystals to represent the Goddess, the moon, and psychic power. Crystals can be used to decorate magickal tools, create protection barriers, and to focus and direct personal power.

Diamond: A highly prized gem of great clarity and brilliance. Diamonds are associated with the sun, the element of fire, and the ability to resonate energy. They are exceptionally hard, resilient, and of course, expensive. Shamans have been known to use diamonds to help them alter their states of consciousness in order to reach higher states of spiritual awareness. The diamond can be worn or carried for protection, courage, wealth, peace, sexual energy, spiritual enlightenment, health, and strength.

Emerald: This brilliant dark green stone is one of the most expensive on the market. It is associated with the goddess Venus and the element of earth. The emerald is used in spells that promote monetary gain, encourage love, and help increase mental powers.

Garnet: A bright red, fiery gem of incredible depth, worn to bestow faithfulness and to renew friendship. The garnet is associated with Mars and the ability to protect. It has been known to enhance bodily strength and virility. Use the garnet for protection, healing, strength, friendship, and love.

Jade: Considered a sacred stone in China, where it is placed on altars to the sun and moon. Jade is also associated with Venus and worn to attract love and marriage. Jade is green in color and can be used for love, healing, longevity, wisdom, and to prolong life.

Jet: Again, this is not a stone but rather fossilized wood, millions of years old. Black as midnight, jet beads are often combined with amber beads and used for protection, psychic power, good luck, and health.

Lapis Lazuli: Prized by the ancient Egyptians for its royal blue color and flecks of golden pyrite. It is associated with the goddesses Isis, Venus, and Ishtar. Lapis brings joy, love, friendship, and courage and helps to protect against infidelity.

Moonstone: An opalescent blue or white feldspar. The moonstone is associated with the Goddess and lunar power. It is worn or carried for love, divination, protection, youth, and healing. Most Witches prize the moonstone above all others because of its connection to the Goddess.

Opal: A very unique gem that contains all the colors of the rainbow. The opal can be used for almost any purpose because of its color range. Ancient myths tell of opals being wrapped in bay leaves and carried to promote invisibility. Opals are used to aid with astral projection, to attract good luck, money, and health, and to convey beauty and power.

Rhodochrosite: A beautiful pink stone that gives off a loving and warm vibration. Rhodochrosite is worn to enhance beauty, to build friendships, and to attract love. It can also be used to reduce stress and fatigue.

Ruby: Long considered the stone of Buddha; varies in color from pink to dark red. The ruby is associated with Mars and the element of fire and is highly prized for its clear color. Rubies are worn or carried for protection, personal power, joy, attraction, wealth, and spirituality.

Sapphire: Considered by magicians to be a very powerful and spiritual stone. It is associated with the god Apollo and is usually worn to stimulate the third eye. The sapphire will attract love, bring visions during meditation, and enhance spiritual activity.

Topaz: Associated with the sun, fire, and the Egyptian god Ra. The yellow topaz is used for protection, healing, or attracting money and great wealth. The blue topaz heightens spiritual awareness and brings peace, harmony, and love.

Turquoise: Highly prized by many North American Indian tribes for its beauty and healing qualities. Its blue-green color is associated with the goddess Venus, the element of earth and the Great Spirit. Turquoise is used for healing, courage, money, protection, and friendship, and is said to bring the wearer good fortune.

Jewel and Gem Magick

A Spell for Confidence and Courage

Use this spell whenever you need for self-confidence, self-esteem, or the courage to handle a difficult situation.

Items needed: One opal pendant and one red candle.

Relax and let go of your fears and tensions. Take several deep breaths and then light the candle. Pick up the opal pendant, hold it in your hands, and feel the power that emanates from within its shimmering depths—where all the colors of the rainbow converge. Take several more deep breaths, feel the power of the opal flow into your hands, and circulate through your entire body. Visualize renewed strength and courage. Hold the opal close to the flame of the candle, as you chant:

Cosmic forces, above and below,
Come to my aid and help me to know.
To find, to seek, to look within,
To overcome insecurities that creep in.
I ask thee now to enter my dreams
And fulfill my desires for self-esteem.
May I now have courage in all that I do.
Let my personal power now shine through.

Focus all your attention on the opal and the candle flame. Repeat the chant two more times. As you do this, feel your personal power grow and strengthen. Visualize yourself as a courageous and determined person. When you feel the time is right, extinguish the candle and wear the opal pendant. You may also use amethyst, diamond, and lapis for courage, strength, and power.

KEY

The key is symbolic of the power to open and the power to lock. This concept is displayed in the symbol of the dove and the key, signifying the spirit that opens the gates of heaven. In Roman mythology, Janus, the god of doors and new beginnings, was generally represented by a doorkeeper's staff and key. The goddess Hecate was the keeper of the key that unlocked the door to the underworld, which opened the way to the mysteries and secrets of knowledge found in the afterlife.

In symbolic language, a key often signifies initiation and the knowledge the owner of the key will soon possess. The color of the key is important as well. The silver key represents psychological understanding, the gold key signifies philosophical wisdom, and the key made of diamond confers the power to act.

To find a key signifies the stage prior to the actual discovery of the treasure, found only after great difficulties. There is also a relationship between the key and the Egyptian ankh (sign of eternal life). We often see engravings of Egyptian gods and goddesses holding the ankh by the top as if it were a key, especially in ceremonies concerning the dead. As an archetypal symbol, the key represents the knowledge or ability to open up the gates of death to immortality.

KNOT

The knot is a symbol of linking, bonding, or the connection to protective powers. The Egyptians used the knot to symbolize life and immortality. The Isis knot, which resembles an ankh with its arms at its sides, was widely used as an amulet of binding and releasing. It represented the ability to hold the power of magick until it was ready to be released.

In magick and Witchcraft, the knot is used in conjunction with the Law of Mimicry and the Law of Similarity sometimes referred to as homeopathic or imitative magick. These laws basically state that like produces like, or that an effect may resemble its cause. Simply put, whatever you do to the symbolic representation of a person, place or thing (such as a Voodoo doll), will directly affect that same person, place, or thing.

It is believed that to conjure up a good etheric intelligence during a healing or protection ritual, and then to knot a cord around the image of the subject being treated, will keep the etheric world helper close to the subject for protection. This same principle is used in knot magick to bind an energy or force to an individual in need, or when untied to release the individual from an affliction or situation.

Knot Magick

Knot magick, sometimes referred to as cord magick, relies mainly on the powers of concentration and visualization. The cord and tying of the knots are points of focus that will link the thought-form to the individual or situation and bind it, or hold it in position. This type of magick is used to stop a person from harming him or herself or another, to stop a situation until it can be dealt with on the material plane; or to bind two people together for the purpose of love and marriage. As with all of magick, the instrument of the act is neutral, leaving the ramifications or outcome the responsibility of the individual performing the work.

Knots of Love Binding Spell

This spell is best used when two people are already in love. I don't recommend this spell to bind people against their will, especially in the case of a separation or divorce.

Items needed: One 9″ length of red cord, photographs of you and the one you desire, two red candles, and a red cloth pouch large enough to hold the bound pictures.

Place all the items on your altar. Take several deep breaths, pick up the picture of your loved one, and look directly at it. Visualize the person in the picture being attentive and loving. Light one candle and say:

With flame and fire
I create desire.
As this spell I fashion
I do bring forth passion.

Take several deep breaths, light the other candle, and repeat:

With flame and fire
I create desire.
As this spell I fashion
I do bring forth passion.

Take the pictures and place them face to face. Hold them close to your heart and visualize the romance, feel the passion between you and the other person. Place the pictures between the two candles. Pick up the cord and tie seven evenly spaced knots in it. With each knot you tie, chant:

By the power of earth and heaven
Turn to me, turn to me by seven.

Pick up the pictures, being sure to keep them face to face, and bind them together with the cord. As you do this, chant with great emotion:

With knot and cord your love and mine
Heart to heart I firmly bind.

Place the bound pictures back on the altar between the candles. When the candles have completely burned out, lovingly place the bound pictures in the red pouch. Keep the pouch with you during the day and place it under your pillow at night.

Protection Binding Spell

If you feel that a specific person is out to do you or others harm, this simple spell should stop them in their tracks.

Items needed: Photograph of the person to be bound, one black candle, one 9″ piece of black cord, and a box filled with dirt.

On the night of the waning moon, collect all the required items. Place them on your altar. At the stroke of midnight begin the spell.

Light the candle and visualize the subject of your spell as you chant:

Black as night and this dark hour
I have the right, I have the power.

Pick up the black cord and tie nine evenly spaced knots in it as you chant:

I bind thee from doing harm,
Your evil now I disarm.
Bound by knot and cord you remain
Until from harm you shall refrain.

Tie the knotted cord around the photo. Place the bound picture in the box and cover it with the dirt. Extinguish the black candle. Bury the box in a safe place. When the individual whose image is resting in the box stops hurting you and others, you may safely take them out of the box and unbind them.

LAMP

The lamp and the lantern are symbolic representations of life, the light of divinity, immortality, the intellect, guidance, and transitions in life. The striking or extinguishing of a lamp signifies the birth or death of someone. Since the lamp brings light to darkness it corresponds to truth and wisdom.

The pottery or earthenware lamp is a symbol of humanity. The oil in the lamp contains the energy to power the lamp. When it is lighted, the spirit of the lamp is born in the flame. Lamps appear in myths and legends and even have a place in divination. The ninth enigma of the Tarot is the hermit, holding his lantern aloft to help guide the fool upon his journey. The promise of the light restores self-confidence and helps maintain good judgment.

LAMP MAGICK

The lamp has four distinct parts. The base of the lamp corresponds to the element of earth and is the foundation upon which you will structure your magickal work. The globe represents the element of air and is a reflection of your intention. The wick that burns becomes the element of fire and is a symbol of your energy, motivation, and power. The oil is equivalent to the element of water and the fluid that sustains your motivation.

The first step in lamp magick is to paint or decorate the lamp base with colors and symbols that reflect your desire. For example, if you were doing a love-drawing spell you might want to paint the base red, with pink and white hearts and then add a heart patterned ribbon.

The globe is the ideal vehicle for magickal expression. Using glass paint, write the name of the one you desire in red paint and your name in pink. Fill in the empty spaces with hearts and flowers. The oil is what empowers or gives life to the wick; it is the source of energy and power that will manifest your desire. For love, you could mix a few drops of rose oil in with red lamp oil to reinforce your intention.

Lamp Oil Colors	
Red	Love, passion, desire, strength, and courage
Yellow	Communication, attraction, persuasion
Green	Money, luck, health, goals, love, marriage
Blue	Creativity, peace, wisdom, psychic ability
Purple	Power, ambition
Clear	Universal, can be used for all general works

A Spell to Rekindle a Friendship

Items needed: Oil lamp with a gold colored or brass base, yellow lamp oil, lemon oil, yellow ribbon, yellow glass paint.

On the bottom of the lamp, write your friend's name and your name and draw the following sigil:

Fill the lamp with yellow lamp oil, add three drops of lemon oil, and allow several hours for the wick to absorb the oil.

Paint several large yellow sunflowers on the globe, and then tie the yellow ribbon around the base of the lamp. Chant the following as you light the lamp:

This flame shall shine by day and night
You will look up and see its light.
To guide you back into my life
And forever banish all anger and strife.

Allow the lamp to burn for three hours. During this time, call your friend and make arrangements for him or her to join you for dinner. One hour before your friend is scheduled to arrive, light the lamp and repeat the chant. Place the lamp in the room where you plan to spend the evening.

LOVE

Since the beginning of time, men and women have sought each other out, spending endless hours searching for ways to win each other's favor, only to discover their love is not being reciprocated. As most of us know, this can be a painful and disappointing experience, one that usually leads us to the door of our local psychic or Witch. Hopefully, the magick this individual will conjure up will help us win the love of the one we desire.

LOVE MAGICK

> **Warning:** Love spells work well to get someone's attention or to give a relationship a chance, but it is unwise to use them to try to hold people against their will. When this is done, the only thing keeping the person with you is the energy of the spell. The first time you forget or aren't able to do the spell, the binding energy is gone and the relationship will wither and die.

The Love Box

Items needed: Small, heart shaped box, love-drawing incense, love-drawing oil, pink candle, parchment paper, pen, rose quartz, some of your own hair, orris root powder, charcoal, and matches.

Perform this spell on the first Friday after the moon turns new. To prepare, center and ground yourself. Light the charcoal. Inscribe upon the parchment that which you specifically desire in a lover. Place some love-drawing incense upon the coals. Dress the pink candle with love drawing oil. While saying:

May the gods of love hear my plea
And bring everlasting love to me!

Light the candle and read your petition aloud, then place the candle on top of the parchment paper. Place more incense upon the coals. Meditate upon your wish, and when finished, read the following:

Hail to thee goddess of love
Shine down on me from above,
Bring now a lover to me
As I will so it shall be.

Let all items remain as they are until the candle has completely burned out. Place the parchment paper in the bottom of the box. On top of the paper drip seven drops of the love-drawing oil. Next place your hair, the rose quartz, some of the orris root powder, and the candle drippings into the box. The box should then be placed where it will be most effective (that is to say, where you will likely come in contact with the person upon whom the spell is cast).

A Smoke and Fire Love Spell

Items needed: One sheet of white parchment paper, love drawing incense (mix together 2 tbsp. each of sandalwood, lavender buds, orris root powder. To the powdered mixture add six drops rose oil and one drop cherry oil), church charcoal and censer, one red and one green candle, basic altar tools.

Try to time this spell with the turning of the moon from new to full.

Before doing the ritual, draw the following symbols on the parchment paper. Place the paper on your altar and set the green candle on the Venus symbol and the red candle on the Mars symbol.

Venus   **Mars**

Begin the ritual by casting the magick circle. Then light the green (Venus) candle as you say:

Lady of love, I appeal to thee.

Light the red (Mars) candle as you say:

Lord of lust, bring him [her] to me.

Light the charcoal. When the coal begins to glow, sprinkle the love-drawing incense on it. Stare into the smoke, visualize the one you desire, and chant the following three times in your most sultry, sexy voice:

The gods of love mine eyes dost kiss
And rise into ether, gather in mist
Then return to Earth, and my love impart
A passion so great as to inflame his [her] heart.

The incense smoke will carry the message to the one you desire, imbuing them with love and desire only for you.

Ancient Gypsy Love Spell

This spell is considered by most Gypsies to be very potent. Timing is the most important ingredient of this spell.

Step One: Cut a blade of grass 7″ long at midnight during the full moon.

Step Two: Before the clock strikes 1 a.m., you must hold the blade of grass in your mouth, face the East, and say:

Before the sun shall rise,
[Insert name] shall here my call.
Before the sun shall set,
[Insert name] for me shall fall.

Step Three: turn to the West and repeat the chant.

Step Four: Cut the grass into small pieces

Step Five: Invite your loved one for dinner. Mix the grass in with his or her food and he or she will fall madly in love with you.

Seven Day Love Spell

Items needed: One red candle at least 8″ long, seven pieces of paper measuring 3″ x 1″, one pen, one knife.

Write the name of the one you desire on each piece of paper. Fold each piece lengthwise twice, so that you have seven pieces of paper 3″ long and about 1/4″ wide. Using the knife, cut six equally spaced notches into the red candle.

Begin this spell seven days before the full moon. Take one of the pieces of folded paper and light one end with a match. Light the candle with the flame from the burning paper. Allow the paper to burn up completely in the candle's flame. As you do this, chant:

By the powers of earth and heaven,
[Insert name] turn to me, turn to me, by seven.

Allow the candle to burn down to the first notch. Repeat the spell each day until the full moon. On the night of the full moon, light the paper, and the candle from the paper, as before, only this time, chant the following:

O lovely lady of the moon,
Grant to me this special boon.
That the one I love shall love only me,
This is what I seek, So Mote It Be.

Stay with the candle until it burns out. The one you love will only have eyes for you.

MANDRAKE (MANDRAGORA)

Shaped like a human being, the mandrake (mandragora) is a plant that has long been associated with Witchcraft. It is highly toxic and produces a narcotic effect when ingested internally—something I do not recommend! The important thing when selecting a mandrake is to find one in the shape of the opposite sex of the person on whom you wish to cast the spell, and then to immediately carve the root into a human form.

There are two genera of plants that are traditionally classified as mandragora: the *mandragora officinalis*, a member of the tomato family (which includes deadly nightshade and devil's apple) and the English white bryony (*bryonia dioica*), which is related to the cucumber and gourd. Both can be used in spells calling for mandrake, but they should be used with great caution, as they are extremely poisonous.

Legend speaks of gathering the mandrake on the night of the full moon as close to the Vernal Equinox as possible. The plant should be carefully extracted from the earth. A small section of the mandrake is clipped away and replanted in the spot from where it was taken. The mandrake is then gently carved into human shape and replanted in either a church yard or at the spot where two paths cross (crossroads). Each night for one lunar month, the mandrake is watered with a combination of distilled water, milk, and a drop of your blood.

When the lunar month has ended, remove the mandrake from the ground. If you've cared for it properly, the mandrake's skin will have completely healed over and taken on human form. To complete the process, you will need to dry the mandrake. This can be done by placing it on a bed of vervain leaves in a warm oven or by passing it through the incense smoke of burning vervain leaves. (Note that the latter method will take months to complete, as the root dries very slowly.) Clothe the mandrake in unbleached muslin and keep near the hearth or in the room you use most frequently. It will serve to bring you health, wealth, and happiness.

METAL

Ever since Vulcan, son of Jupiter, created thunderbolts in his underground forge, the power of metal magick as been a closely guarded secret. In Western alchemy it was believed that the metals found on earth were influenced by their corresponding planetary rulers. Each metal was then named after a planet, imbued with the planet's attributes, and incorporated into daily life through the days of the week. By using the corresponding metal, one was supposed to be able to control the forces that prevailed each day.

PLANETARY QUALITIES OF METALS

Gold: The metal of the sun, gold governs Sunday and is associated with strength, power, success, achievement, wealth, and masculine energy.

Silver: The metal of the moon, silver governs Monday and is associated with the feminine mystique, intuition, instinctive wisdom, spiritual and psychic understanding, fertility, and magick.

Iron: The metal of Mars, iron governs Tuesday and is associated with war and aggression. It also stands against injustice and exudes masculine force and power.

Mercury: The metal of Mercury, it governs Wednesday and is associated with communication, business, selling oneself and being heard. It holds the power of influence.

Tin: The metal of Jupiter, tin governs Thursday and is associated with wisdom, idealism, expansion, and ambition. It is good for legal problems and career, and is a masculine force.

Copper: The metal of Venus, it governs Friday and matters of the heart, love, emotions, lust, sex, and fertility. It is good for relationships and health and is a totally feminine force.

Lead: The metal of Saturn, lead governs Saturday and is associated with change, transition, formation through restriction, and learning through trial and error. It is considered to be related to the first law of Karma: limitation.

METAL MAGICK

Gold Money Magick

Items needed: Gold filings or nuggets, small dish, sunflower petals, and 10 coins.

Place the dish in the sunlight. Focus your attention on the dish. Visualize the dish filling with money, cascading over the edge like a waterfall of gold. See in your mind's eye gold, coins, and money filling the room where the dish is. Each day place a new coin in the dish. In time you will begin to generate money-making ideas. Each time you place a coin in the dish, your will to create wealth will increase and so will your success and prosperity.

The Copper Love Charm

Items needed: Seven copper pennies, one copper bracelet, one green candle, and a green velvet pouch.

Begin on the night of the new moon. Place all the items called for on your altar. Cast the magick circle, and light the green candle as you say:

Power of Venus on this night
Work my will by candlelight
Bring to me the one I see
As I will So Mote It Be.

Place the copper bracelet in the green pouch. Take one copper penny, kiss it, and say the following:

Bright and shining one of love,
Descend to me from above.
Attend to me and work my will,
With great passion my love fulfill.
By my side forever strong,
For this is what I crave and long.

Put the penny in the pouch along with the bracelet. Lay the pouch next to the candle. Allow the candle to burn for one hour. Extinguish the candle and cut a door in your circle, but do not take it up or disturb the altar arrangement. Repeat the spell for six consecutive nights. On the last night allow the candle to burn out. Fashion a heart from the left-over wax and push all the pennies into it. Put the heart in a safe place. The following day present your loved one with the bracelet, and he or she will be yours forever.

Iron Protection Ritual

Items needed: Eight pieces of iron or iron nails, one black candle, a dish of salt, and protection incense.

Place the candle on the floor near your front door. Encircle the candle with the iron pieces and then with a ring of salt. Place the dish of salt on the outside of the circle to the west of the candle. Light the incense and walk around your house with it as you say:

Let that which is unwanted be gone,
Never to return from this moment on.

Return to the circle and light the black candle as you say:

Into the flame, into the fire
Burns all that I do not desire.
To be purified by earth and salt
Evil energies now halt.

Allow the candle and incense to burn out. Sprinkle the pieces of iron or nails around the outside perimeter of your home or apartment.

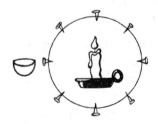

MIRROR

The mirror signifies truth, self-knowledge, wisdom, and the soul. It is considered to be a reflection of the supernatural or divine intelligence behind creativity. The mirror also symbolizes the moon, due to its ability to reflect light. Magickally, the mirror can be used to divine the future, create protective devices, and look into your own nature.

The art of divining the future by gazing into a mirror appears throughout the history of western mysticism. A devotee of the goddess Demeter gazed into a sacred spring and predicted the harvest. It is believed that Catherine de Medici, a reputed Witch, depended on mirror divination to guide her through the tangled affairs of state in 16th century France. Directions for divining the future can be found in the *Grimorium Verum*, published in 1517.

MIRROR MAGICK

Mirror Gazing

The most versatile mirror for augury is full length, has three panels, and provides a view of three sides of an image at once. When this triple reflective quality is combined with candlelight, it creates a very mystical effect.

A full moon night is advised for scrying. Stand the mirror in the corner of a darkened room and place a lighted candle before each panel. Position a chair facing the center panel. Sit in the chair, take several deep breaths, and relax. Stare fixedly at the reflected image of the center candle flame, pose your question, and look deep into the mirror. The mirror will begin to cloud or fog with a swirling veil of ethereal mist. Through the mist, an image will appear and answer your query. When the image begins to fade, so will the mist. Once the mirror is clear, extinguish the candles, cover the mirror with a dark blue or black velvet drape, and record the message in your book of shadows.

The Mirror Box

There comes a time in everyone's life when protection is needed from outside negative forces. This is especially true for those involved in Witchcraft and the magickal arts. For some reason, it seems to be the delight of neophyte Witches to psychically attack their peers solely for the sheer delight of doing it. In such cases, where ignorance is the motive, the offending individual warrants some time in the mirror box.

The mirror box is a reflective tool for turning one's own spitefulness against others. There is no need to thrust pins in a doll, invoke the demons of hell, or call upon the grim reaper. A simple returning of negativity will suffice. Use common sense and think before you act. This doesn't mean you must turn the other cheek, or become a living martyr, but rather be reasonable and don't join your rivals in the gutter.

How To Make The Mirror Box

Items needed: One medium sized box with a lid, black construction paper or paint, six mirror tiles, one black candle, sandalwood oil, and a photograph of or handwriting sample from the person to be placed in the box.

Paper or paint the outside of the box black. Cut the mirror tiles to fit the inside of the box's lid, sides, and bottom. Glue them in place with the reflective sides facing inward so when you look into the box you are able to see your reflection.

Begin this spell on a Thursday night just before the moon turns new. Place the box on a table facing the direction where your enemy lives. Dress the candle with sandalwood oil as you chant:

It is not to hate or burn,
Just your evil to return.

Place the candle on top of the box and lean the photograph or handwriting against it. Light the candle. Focus your attention on the photograph to create a mental link with the person and chant:

All that is evil and sent to me
Is reflected back and returned to thee.
This magickal box shall hold you tight
As your evilness turns against you this night.
All that you have sent to me
Shall now be returned by law of three.

Lift the candle off the box, being careful not to extinguish it. Open the box and place the picture inside. Close the lid and replace the candle on top of the box. Allow the candle to burn for one hour. Repeat this spell for three consecutive nights. On the third night, seal the box shut with wax from the candle, then allow the black candle to burn out. Bury the box or store it in a safe place. If the person in the box continues to vex you, repeat the spell.

MOON

The moon, like the sun, rises in the East and sets in the West. Unlike the sun, the appearance of its size and shape continually change, at least from our earth-bound perspective. In a lunar month there are four cycles of approximately seven days. The phases the moon goes through include the dark of the moon (also called the new moon). It waxes (grows larger) until the first quarter is visible as the half moon. When the moon continues to wax, its horns point to the East until it reaches a full circle, known as the full moon. It will then begin to diminish in size as it wanes through the last quarter, with the horns pointing West, and continues to wane until the new moon returns.

| Dark (new) | First Quarter | Full | Last Quarter |

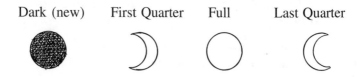

It is wise to time your magickal rites to coincide with the proper phase of the moon. By doing this you take advantage of lunar power, stay in sympathy with the natural pull of the universe, and combine your energy with nature's. The more circumstances you can bring into alignment when doing magick, the better the results will be.

Use the waxing moon to begin new projects, build friendships, rekindle a romance, and create new business opportunities. During the full moon, nurture and reaffirm intentions, focus energy on projects set in motion during the new moon, and work to create success and abundance.

During the dark or waning moon, take time to reflect on goals and ambitions. Use this time to break undesirable habits and patterns and to undo negative influences coming from others.

Moon Magick

Full Moon Blessing Rite

Items needed: Clear glass bowl, a one-liter bottle of spring water, silver paint, sprig of jasmine, moonstone, two white altar candles, gardenia incense and oil, small paint brush, and usual altar tools.

Use the silver paint to inscribe the following symbol on the outside bottom of the bowl:

Set your altar so the light of the full moon shines directly on it. Fill the bowl with the spring water. Place the bowl and all the other items called for on the altar. Cast your magick circle and then light the altar candles, saying:

Lady I now invite thee here
As the mother of sacred Earth,
Whose power is beyond compare
When dreams are given birth.

Hold the moonstone and sprig of jasmine in offering as you ask this blessing:

Lady of desire, reflection of light
You are my motion, direction, and second sight.
Mother of creation, the original source,
You are potential, power, the ultimate force.
Grandmother of time, wise one from above,
I summon thee here with honor and love.

Gently place the moonstone and sprig of jasmine in the water. Pick up the bowl and hold it in offering as you say:

I call the brilliant evening star,
The virgin of celestial light.
The gracious goddess from afar,
Great mother of second sight.

Glorious queen of the twilight hour
Wise and vigilant protector,
Thou whose silent power
Is regal and most splendor.

I beckon thee to now descend
Great mystery behind the veil
She who rises time and again
The keeper of the grail.

Set the bowl down. Anoint your forehead with a drop of the water. Extinguish the candles, take up the circle, and carefully place the bowl in a window where the moon will continue to shine on it. Just before sunrise, remove the jasmine and stone. Pour the contents of the bowl into a bottle with a lid, and close tightly. Keep the moonstone with your other magickal tools. Take the jasmine to the nearest river or lake, toss it in the water as you make a wish. Use the moon water to bless and consecrate your circle, or in place of oil to anoint candles and other magickal objects.

Waxing Moon Money Spell

Items needed: One silver candle, 1 tsp. ground allspice, almond oil.

On the night of the waxing moon, inscribe the silver candle with the exact amount of money you need. Rub the candle with the almond oil as you chant the following:

As the moon doth wax and grow
So to me doth money flow.

Once you feel the candle is thoroughly charged with your wish, roll it in the allspice and light. Allow the candle to burn for one hour and then extinguish. Repeat this spell each night, at the same time, until the moon is full. On the night of the full moon allow the candle to burn out.

Full Moon Love Spell

Items needed: One red candle and one white candle, 1 tsp. each of ginseng, jasmine, and lovage, three drops each of rose oil, lavender oil, and violet oil, a small white plate, a piece of parchment paper, and one 9″ strip of red ribbon.

On the day of the full moon, melt the red candle in a double boiler. When the wax has melted, mix in the herbs and oils. Remove the pan from the stove and stir the wax as it begins to cool. Chant the following over the wax.

Mother of the moon, goddess of love,
Descend to me from far above.
Within this wax passion inspire
That I shall have the one I desire.

When the wax has cooled, but not solidified, dip the white candle in it so that the herbal wax mixture thoroughly coats the candle. Allow the candle to dry.

Then, beneath the full moon, inscribe your name on one side of the candle and the name of the one you desire on the opposite side of the candle. Hold the candle to your heart as you repeat the previous chant. Fill the candle with all your love and desire. When you feel the candle has been thoroughly charged, light it. Visualize you and the one your desire together. Allow the candle to burn out.

Waning Moon Protection Charm

Items needed: One tsp. each patchouli, sandalwood, and clove, an incense brazier, self-igniting charcoal, and a small white stone inscribed with the following protection sigil:

When the moon is no longer visible, place a piece of charcoal in your brazier and light it. Mix the herbs together and sprinkle them over the glowing coal. As the mixture begins to burn, pass the stone through the smoke, as you chant:

Within this stone
I pass my plight,
Banished forever
From this night.

Take the stone to the nearest body of moving water. Toss the stone in and walk away.

NUMEROLOGY

Numerology is believed to be one of the oldest forms of divination. The ancient Egyptians and Babylonians held theories of the occult significance of numbers. During the Middle Ages, numbers were especially important to the Kabbalists, whose mystical system was based on a numerical system called gematria and the 22 letters of the Hebrew alphabet.

However, it was the Greek mathematician and philosopher Pythagoras who made the biggest impact on numerical theory. He believed that the whole universe was ordered mathematically, and that everything in it could be expressed in terms of numbers. He considered numbers to be the key to the universe.

The basis of numerology is the belief that the numbers from one to nine exert an influence on our lives and personalities. Each letter in the alphabet is therefore assigned a numerical value from one through nine. When a person's name is spelled out, the numerical values can be seen and then reduced to a single digit. Studying the numbers in a person's name reveals inclinations in love, health, vocation, and spirituality. Although numerology relies on mathematical configurations to construct personal profiles, it is far easier to learn than astrology.

NUMBERS AND THEIR MEANINGS

One: Number one stands for all that is strong, individual, and creative. Number one people have an unswerving drive towards achievement. They are powerful characters, positive and self-reliant, and can be assertive. Most ones are ambitious and aggressive. They have excellent powers of concentration and good memories, and are natural born leaders and inventors.

As they are extremely independent, ones tend to work better by themselves. However, a one can be obstinate, and usually refuses to listen to or follow advice from subordinates. Forceful and untiring, ones try to dominate everyone around them, sometimes to the point of tyranny. They are, essentially, people who look after number one. If their egos are not kept in check, they can become very selfish and willful.

Two: Number two people are gentle, passive, and artistic, and have soft, sweet natures. Twos are even-tempered lovers of peace and harmony. They are especially tidy and modest. The two is usually a follower rather than a leader, and when twos do get their way, it is usually through persuasion and diplomacy.

The number two person usually understands both sides of a situation, so much so that he or she shifts back and forth, never reaching a satisfactory decision. The two will likely change his or her mind frequently and put things off indefinitely. The very sense of judgment that enables them to give good advice to friends often prevents twos from making up their own minds. However, with the right friends and associates, they will go far.

Three: A three person is brilliant, imaginative, versatile, and energetic. Threes just seem to sparkle and glitter. They tend to express their ideas boldly, and with great enthusiasm. They have keen, intuitive minds and can learn quickly. However, threes have a tendency to take on too much, spread their energy in too many directions at once, and then not finish what they have started.

Witty, lively, and charming, they are likely to become successful in life, especially in the arts or spiritual endeavors. Threes tend to be lucky and seem to succeed without really trying. The three has fantastic potential and loves to be in control and tell others what to do.

Four: A four person is earth-oriented, solid, and practical. Fours may seem to lack the spark of the more creative vibrations because of their efficiency. They are down-to-earth, calm, steady, and respectable, the pillars of society. They are cautious and don't take risks.

Though fours are able to grasp new ideas quickly, they prefer to study them before making any decisions.

Four people like routine and detailed work. They make great technicians and researchers. Unfortunately, fours tend to be grim, repressive, suspicious, and resentful of anyone whose ways are not like theirs. The four usually gains friends through honest, hard work, dependability, and constant effort. Fours will always keep on plugging, and they always finish what they start.

Five: The five is restless, jumpy, clever, and impatient. Fives live off their nerves and coffee. They are ambitious and love to travel, meet new people, and be in different surroundings. People with this vibration are capable, quick, and willing to accept new ideas. They seem to be Jacks-of-all-trades. The unusual and bizarre fascinate fives, who enjoy gambling, speculation, and risks. They make excellent salespeople.

Fives are adventurous, attractive, and quick tempered. They live for the moment and detest responsibility and mundane activities. They hate to be tied down and committed to routine tasks. Their lively nature tends to make them a bit conceited and sarcastic. The five would rather learn the hard way than take advice from others, which usually leads to setbacks and even misfortune and loss.

Six: Six is the number of harmony, domesticity, and peaceful happiness. They have a great talent for friendship, home, and family life. Sixes are kind, reliable, and well-balanced individuals. These are the true homemakers. They just seem to have the ability to get along with everyone—no matter what their race, religion, or creed. Sixes love beauty, warmth, and, above all, home and family. They appreciate the cultured life and gravitate toward music, art, poetry, and sculpture.

Sixes are loyal, conscientious, idealistic, and affectionate. They are often called upon to fill positions of trust, and generally live up to the expectations of others. If they do not find fame, it is because they have become satisfied with what they already have, and don't reach for higher pinnacles. Let a six run your business. He or she will have a way of attracting followers and customers, and will usually be socially prominent in the community.

Seven: Seven is the scholar, philosopher, and mystic. Intuition is a strong part of a seven's highly imaginative nature. Sevens love the mysterious and anything to do with the occult side of nature. Composers, musicians, students, philosophers, and mystics are nurtured by this number. The seven tends to withdraw from the world, inspired by solitude. However, Sevens hate obscurity, and will usually blame the world for their failure to gain prominence. Although sevens are capable of solving intricate problems, they seldom understand or really know themselves.

The seven has a penetrating intellect, hidden beneath a dreamy facade that makes them seem fey and strange. Often extraordinarily bad at explaining themselves, they can be very frustrating, especially when they get upset at being questioned. If the they can avoid being pessimistic, aloof, and always disappointed, they will become great teachers and leaders—sevens naturally inspire loyalty.

Eight: Eight stands for power, money, and worldly involvement. Eight is the number of material success—the steady builder of vast commercial and industrial development. The eight puts plans into action, completes them, and then goes on to something bigger. Eights are strong and forceful. They always demand and get the most from others. Opposition does not stop them, and they can be ruthless with rivals and subordinates.

Strong, practical people, eights make successful businessmen and politicians. They work hard, accumulate money, and conduct their operations with caution and tenacity. Eight spells success with dollar marks (*$UCCE$$*), and thrives on progress. The weakness with this number lies in petty jealousies, wasted efforts, and indulgence. The eight can easily become hard, materialistic, and tyrannical. But, when it comes to money, eights have the true Midas touch.

Nine: The number nine combines influence with intellect. Romantic, passionate, and impulsive, nines are people of wide sympathies and great charm. They make brilliant scientists, teachers, and artists. Strong-willed, wild, unorthodox, and impractical, they are always interesting. However, they can be uncharitable and intolerant when opposed.

More often than not, nines become so involved with their humanitarian efforts that they overlook the feelings of those around them. Impatient and impulsive, they move fast and have explosive tempers. If opposed, they are very uncharitable and intolerant. The only time they are cautious is when money is involved, but even then their impulsive nature may give way to generosities not in their best interest. If nines can learn control and balance there is nothing they cannot do or achieve.

NUMEROLOGY ANALYSIS

To analyze an individual using numerology, begin with the date of birth number. This represents the subject's inborn characteristics and is known as the personality number. Next you will want to analyze the name number by which your subject is best known. It will show traits developed during life. Your subject's inner nature is best expressed by the vowel number and is considered to be the number of underlying influence.

To find a person's primary date of birth number, you must add all the numbers of the birth date together until you have a single digit number. For example, is you were born on May 1, 1950, you would first have to reduce May to a number. May is the 5th month, or 5. You would then add up all the numbers: $5 + 1 + 1 + 9 + 5 + 0 = 21$. The 21 is then reduced to a single digit: $2 + 1 = 3$. Your birth number would be 3, and this is the definition you would consult.

The Number Chart								
1	2	3	4	5	6	7	8	9
A	B	C	D	E	F	G	H	I
J	K	L	M	N	O	P	Q	R
S	T	U	V	W	X	Y	Z	

The next step is to analyze the name numerically. To do this you convert the letters of the name into numbers using the number-letter equivalents listed on the chart above. For example, John Smith:

J   O   H   N   S   M   I   T   H
$1 + 6 + 8 + 5 + 1 + 4 + 9 + 2 + 8 = 44 = 4 + 4 = 8$

The primary number for the name John Smith is 8, so you would read the qualities associated with the number eight to find out what traits John has developed throughout his life. If the date of birth number and the name number coincide, the individual will have a pretty smooth life. If they are in opposition to each other it may indicate inner conflict and problems.

The last thing to do is reduce the vowels in the person's name to one digit. This will show what influences are at work beneath the surface.

Oils

The sense of smell is one of the most powerful senses humans have. Connected on a primal level to the unconscious, smell reacts without your conscious knowledge or will. Tied to memory, scent can bring pleasure, alert to danger, cause revulsion, and affect health. Every odor that you perceive causes a chemical reaction in the brain, triggering instincts rather than conscious actions. This is why oils and incense have a prominent place in most magickal operations: They automatically activate responses, bypassing the reasoning self.

Fragrant oils are used to enhance magickal rites, to anoint candles, and to bless and concrete objects, and can even be burned in place of incense. Worn on the body, oils can trigger a sensual, come hither state of mind or a don't come any closer, protective vibration. When oil is used in combination with ritual bathing, it relaxes the body and invigorates the mind, preparing it for magickal work.

The blending of magickal oils is simple and requires little equipment other than an eye dropper, essential oils, and small bottles for storage. If you wish to create your own special blend, be sure the ingredients complement each other and reflect the desired goal. To enhance the effectiveness of your oil, add a crystal, semiprecious stone, flower, seed, or leaf to the bottle. Always be sure to label the bottle according to its purpose and date of creation.

Oil Fragrance Categories

Sweet	Sour	Musky	Woodsy
Vanilla	Orange	Musk	Sandalwood
Heliotrope	Lemon	Dark Musk	Rosewood
Violet	Lime	Patchouli	
Myrrh	Verbena	Civet	**Flowery**
			Rose
Spicy	**Fruity**	**Minty**	Wisteria
Carnation	Fruit of Life	Peppermint	Jasmine
Allspice	Cherry	Spearmint	Gardenia
Cinnamon	Orange	Balm	Honeysuckle
Bayberry	Apple	Sage	Tuberose
Lavender	Pineapple		Magnolia
Bergamot			

Standard Magickal Oil Recipes

Love-Drawing Oil
1 pair Adam and Eve roots
1 part rose oil
1 part cherry oil
1 part musk oil
1 part narcissus oil

Money-Drawing Oil
2 parts apricot oil base
2 parts cinnamon oil
2 parts clove oil
2 parts frankincense oil
1 small high John root in bottle

Power Oil
2 parts safflower oil
2 parts sandalwood oil
2 parts orange oil
2 parts pine oil
2 parts blue sonata
1 garnet
1 ruby

Desire Me Oil
2 parts white musk oil
2 parts jasmine oil
2 parts lotus oil
 2 parts violet oil
1 rose quartz in bottle

Crown of Success Oil
2 parts sunflower oil
2 parts orange oil
2 parts allspice oil
2 parts ambergris oil
Add gold glitter to bottle

Protection Oil
2 parts patchouli oil
2 parts sandalwood oil
2 parts frankincense oil
2 parts verbena oil
1 onyx chip
1 wormwood leaf or stem

P

PENTACLE

No other symbol is more widely associated with Witch-craft than the pentacle, a round disk engraved with a penta-gram (five-pointed star). The circle surrounding the pentagram is the universal symbol of totality. The penta-gram itself symbolizes the human microcosm. It also repre-sents the five elements: Air, Fire, Water, Earth, and Spirit. Upright (as pictured), the pentacle depicts the spirit above matter and is a symbol of the Goddess. Inverted, it corre-sponds to matter above spirit, the quest for temporal gain, and the Horned God of materialism.

In the practice of magick, the pentacle represents the practitioners' ability to create or manifest desire. As the embodiment of the element of Earth and the realm of mate-rialism, the pentacle provides a place, like an artist's canvas, on which abstract thought forms can be brought to life. From a spiritual or esoteric viewpoint, the pentacle represents the realm of birth, life, death, and renewal.

During a magickal operation, practitioners use the symbol of the pentacle to help conceptualize their thoughts, believing that what they see in their minds' eyes they will surely realize in physical form. The pentacle becomes the point of focus where all the practitioner's attention is directed. If practitioners are totally focused and are able to force their will toward a single purpose, they will achieve results and make manifest their desires.

The true beauty and power of the pentacle lies in its versatility. It provides the practitioner with a mode of expression and a place to arrange his or her thought forms until they can be forced into reality. For example, by placing the logo or symbol of your coven or lodge on the pentacle and charging the logo during ritual, you endow those affiliated with the group a portion of the energy raised. This is especially helpful during fund-raising campaigns or when trying to recruit new members.

PHYSICAL PROPERTIES OF THE PENTACLE

When performing a magickal rite, it is important that the symbols you use convey your objective. As an agency of the Earth element, the pentacle makes the ideal surface on which to place your symbolic representations during ritual. Because the pentacle will be serving as the host to your magickal objectives, it is important to consider the physical properties of the pentacle itself. These include: the substance you make your pentacle from, color, and inscriptions or engravings.

Wood

Wood is symbolic of the mother, the Goddess, and wisdom. Wood makes an ideal pentacle, and is very easy to work with. Wood absorbs and radiates energy, infusing the focused thought forms into the objects placed upon it. Choose the wood for your pentacle according to the natural vibrations you would like it to have.

Apple: Belongs to Aphrodite, Venus, Freya, Ishtar, Cerridwen, and the element of Water; used for love, passion, fertility, foundation, and inspiration.

Ash: Corresponds to the gods Neptune, Odin, and Mercury and the elements of Air and Water; aids in mental clarity.

Birch: Associated with the mysteries of the Goddess; the elements of Earth, Air, and Water; is used in making parchment; contributes to health, healing, and general magick.

Hawthorn: Belongs to Mars, Thor, Blodeuwedd, and Hera; the elements of Fire and Earth; allows access to the underworld; is protective, cleansing, and helps to manifest desire.

Hazel: Equates with Mercury, Hermes, Woden, and Thor; the elements of Air and Water; is associated with dowsing, divination, finding hidden things, and developing wisdom.

Maple: Corresponds to Jupiter; the element of Air; promotes love, longevity, and material success.

Oak: Associated with Zeus, Thor, Juno, Diana, Rhea, Demeter, Dagda, Bridget; the elements of Fire and Earth, and sometimes Water; permits entrance into the mysteries, is a keeper of knowledge, and promotes courage, spiritual strength, and protection.

Pine: Aligns with Mars, Freya, Osiris, Cybele; the element of Fire; helps with birth, purification, insight, and divination.

Metal

Metals are the bones of the Earth; the reflection of the powers of the God and Goddess. Metals are beautiful, they conduct energy, and they were considered to be sacred in ancient times. In addition to their temporal qualities, each metal is aligned with a planetary energy that influences all it comes in contact with. Most New Age and Occult shops carry a variety of planetary pentacles for practitioners to choose from. The following six metals are most often used in the construction of altar pentacles.

Silver: Associated with the Moon, Artemis, Selene, Hecate, Diana, Sin, Shiva; the element of Water; encourages the feminine mystique, intuition, instinctive wisdom, spiritual and psychic understanding, fertility, and magick.

Gold: Belongs to the Sun, Apollo, Dionysius, Helios, Sol, Vishnu, Ra; the element of Fire; develops strength, power, success, achievement, wealth, and masculine energy.

Copper: Corresponds to Venus, Aphrodite, Ishtar, Lakshmi, Bast; the elements Water and Fire; aids with matters of the heart, love, passion, friendship, reconciliation of differences, harmony, beauty, and attraction.

Tin: Associated with Jupiter, Zeus, Athens, Poseidon, Minerva, Marduk, and Indra; the element of Water; helps with idealism, expansion, attracting success, obtaining justice, religious leadership, and prosperity.

Iron: Belongs to Mars, Volcanus, Durga, and Sekhmet; the element of Fire; supports dynamic energy, enthusiasm, courage, bodily strength, and war.

Lead: Corresponds to Saturn, Hera, Kronos, Saeturnus, Parvati, Kali, and Ptah; the element of Earth; encourages creativity, the bringing of ideas into material form, restriction, formation, discipline.

Stone

Stone is the symbol of stability, durability, immorality, cohesion, and the indestructibility of the supreme reality.

Stones often accompany trees in sacred places, or stand alone to mark a sacred place or event. The Stone of Foundation is the rock on which the universe was founded, the keystone of the Earth and source of the waters of life, the rock that prevails against Hades and the powers of the underworld. The stones listed here are ones that usually come in slices or sections large enough to fashion into a pentacle.

Agate: Associated with Mercury; the elements of Earth and Fire; helps to build courage, strength, and self healing, is good for protection.

Beryl: Corresponds to Neptune, Tiamat, Mara; the element of Water; can be used for healing, love, and to stop gossip.

Calcite: Equates with Venus; the element of Water, aids in centering, spiritual endeavors, purification, protections, and healing.

Geodes: Associated with the Great Mother; the element of Water; are used for meditation and fertility.

Malachite: Corresponds to Venus; the element of Earth; is good to use for love, peace, business success , and power.

Petrified Wood: Is not an actual stone but rather a fossil that is associated with the Akasha and the elements; most often used for past-life regression, healing, and protection.

Planets

Millions of years old, from ancient Babylon to modern times, the planets have always symbolized the essential forces of the universe. Equated with the gods, endowed with magickal attributes, and viewed as lights of influence, then and now the planets affect all aspects of daily life.

The sun and the moon, which dominated the daylight hours and night skies, were the first "planets" to be associated with the life-giving forces of the elements, seasons, and man's day-to-day struggle to survive. These two luminaries were credited with the power to control the cyclic process and deified as the source of life itself.

As mythology and storytelling evolved, so did the god-like qualities of the celestial bodies, and their ability to control human existence. Besides the sun and moon, the father and mother of the universe, other planetary gods and goddesses began to emerge, each with his or her own individual identity and domain of influence.

The sun, moon, Mars, Mercury, Jupiter, Venus, and Saturn (the sun and moon are regarded as planets in this sense) formed the original pantheon of heavenly powers that ruled over the affairs of humans. Each planet was assigned an area of influence that controlled the human endeavors within that realm. For example, the Sun was equated with the Greek god Apollo, and governed strength, self-expression, and vitality, which were associated with leadership, royalty, and government.

Learning to use planetary energy makes magickal work easier, since each planet relates to everyday life in some way. Basically, just about everything we do or seek to achieve is subordinate to a planetary force. Magickally, this means that everything in creation responds to a specific planetary energy. Therefore, if you know which energy rules or governs a certain object or event, then you can use the corresponding planetary power to influence it. The more you know about the planets and their corresponding attributes and symbols, the more precise you can be in designing magickal rites.

Planetary Correspondences

Sun

Glyph	☉
Symbols	Hexagram, diadem, alchemical crucible
Deities	Apollo, Sol, Dionysos, Helios, Bridget, Aine, Macha
Archangel	Michael
Day	Sunday
Colors	Gold, yellow
Numbers	One or six
Metal	Gold
Stones	Diamond, amber, clear quartz, topaz
Incense	Frankincense, sandalwood
Plant	Bay, cinnamon, heliotrope, marigold, orange
Trees	Oak, pine
Animals	Lion, hawk, bull

The sun is authoritative, creative, courageous, and healing. With its life-giving warmth, the sun is at the center of existence, and whatever exists at the center will activate what is at the perimeter. It is primarily associated with will power, activity, authority, and leadership. The sun should be used to acquire self-esteem, attract fame and material success, encourage physical strength and courage, aid physical healing, and assist with political ambition.

Moon

Glyph	☽
Symbols	Crescent, cup, silver sickle
Deities	Hecate, Selene, Diana, Thoth
Archangel	Gabriel
Day	Monday
Colors	Silver, white,
Number	Two
Metal	Silver

Stones	Moonstone, pearl, chalcedony, mother of pearl
Incense	Jasmine, lotus, ylang-ylang
Plants	Lily, hyacinth, iris, narcissus
Trees	Willow, hawthorn
Animals	Crab, owl, vulture, horse

There are more myths and legends about the moon than any other planetary body. The moon just seems to ignite the imagination and quicken the mystical senses. Lighting the night sky, the moon allows us to see past reality and into the shadows of night. The moon is receptive, reflects the light of the sun, and governs our physical and emotional responses. Lunar magick works best when it is used to learn control over emotions, create passion, assist with glamour-magick, and increase intuition and psychic abilities.

Mars

Glyph	♂
Symbols	Pentagram, lance, scourge
Deities	Mars, Volcanus, Durga, Sekhmet
Archangel	Samuel
Day	Tuesday
Colors	Red, burgundy
Number	Five
Metal	Iron
Stones	Bloodstone, flint, onyx, garnet, ruby
Incense	Dragonsblood, galangal, tobacco
Plants	Bloodroot, ginger, snapdragon, nettle
Trees	Rowan, ash, pepper tree
Animals	Ram, wolf, scorpion, salamander

Mars is dynamic energy, enthusiasm, and resolution. It rules personal expression, character, and bodily strength. Mars represents action and it induces humans to take risks and to rush into things before thinking. The key image of Mars is force—pushing and shoving to fit with little regard

for right or wrong. Under the rulership of this planet we
find a instinctive need to lead, to survive, and to clear the
path of all obstacles that stand in the way of personal
accomplishment. Mars energy should be used to build
strength of character, reinforce determination, confront enemies, and win battles.

Mercury

☿

Glyph	
Symbol	Caduceus, scroll, stylus
Deities	Hermes, Mercurius, Thoth,
Archangel	Raphael
Day	Wednesday
Colors	Yellow, orange, apricot
Number	Eight
Metals	Mercury (quicksilver), zinc
Stones	Citrine, agate
Incense	Styrax (liquid storax), gum arabic, lavender
Plants	Lavender, marjoram, star anise, bittersweet
Trees	Birch, aspen, almond
Animals	Fox, cheetah, baboon, ostrich, carrier pigeon

Mercury is symbolically related to communication and
the ability to think. It governs the human potential to
reason, make decisions, evaluate situations, and analyze facts.
Creative thinking, rational thinking, and original thinking
are unique to humans, setting us apart from the animal kingdom. Thinking is a powerful tool and carries with it a tremendous amount of responsibility. All people are responsible
for using their minds in an honorable manner and for the
betterment of all living things. Mercury should be used to
enhance the thought process, remove stress, tension, and
depression, and increase creativity and original thinking.

Jupiter

Glyph	♃
Symbols	Thunderbolt, trident, crown
Deities	Zeus, Athena, Jupiter, Minerva, Tinia, Marduk, Maat
Archangel	Sachiel
Day	Thursday
Colors	Purple, dark blue
Number	Four
Metal	Tin
Stones	Amethyst, lepidolite, sugilite
Incense	Pine, sandalwood, clove
Plants	Borage, sage, betony, nutmeg
Tree	Juniper, cedar, pine, sycamore
Animals	Whale, swan, eagle

Jupiter corresponds to knowledge, understanding, good judgment, and prosperity. It rules the concepts of expansion, opportunity, and good fortune. Jupiter is a joyful planet that promotes abundance through realistic effort and hard work. One thing that Jupiter helps people do is change their attitudes from a negative to positive. Once the attitude changes, so does everything else, because if you have a positive frame of mind you can accomplish just about anything. Use Jupiter to attract wealth and great riches, build dignity, acquire wisdom and make good judgments, improve moral values, increase financial health, and expand knowledge and understanding of religious and philosophical concepts.

Venus

Glyph	♀
Symbols	Mirror, girdle, shell
Deity	Venus, Aphrodite, Ishtar, Lakshmi, Bast
Archangel	Anael
Day	Friday
Colors	Green, turquoise, luminescent greenish white

Number	Seven
Metal	Copper
Stone	Emerald, jade, lapis lazuli, chrysocolla, coral
Incense	Rose, lilac, violet
Plants	Rose, iris, orchid, orris, passion flower, vanilla
Trees	Apple, cherry, avocado, fig
Animals	Lynx, cat, rabbit, dove, sparrow

Venus is the epitome of the feminine mystique, the queen of love and beauty. Venus offers what others cannot, the quality of simple abundance. All of nature responds to Venus and the pleasures she affords. Passion, peace, affection, money, success, and friendships all come under the rule of Venus. Use Venus to arouse the passions of a loved one, create a peaceful environment, acquire money, become successful, and gain new friendships.

Saturn

Glyph	♄
Symbols	Scythe, key, double axe
Deities	Saturn, Kronos, Hera, Kali, Net
Archangel	Cassiel
Day	Saturday
Color	Black
Number	Three
Metal	Lead
Stones	Onyx, obsidian, jet, hematite, apache tear
Incense	Patchouli, Myrrh
Plants	Belladonna, hemlock, ladyslipper, yew
Trees	Beech, yew, elm, ebony, cypress
Animals	Goat, spider, goose, bat

Saturn is the planet of stability and restriction. Its energies test our balance and endurance. In some ways Saturn symbolizes time, which, with its ravenous appetite for life, devours all its creations. Saturn, like time, brings restlessness, the sense of duration lasting from the moment of stimulus up to the peak of satisfaction. Saturn is slow, deliberate, disciplined success. Use Saturn to improve concentration, discipline a lazy mind, become better at work, and motivate yourself.

Each one of the seven planets produces a different energy field or vibration that can be used to enhance magickal operations. By incorporating this energy into your magickal works, you increase their effectiveness. For example, a love-drawing ritual would have tremendous impact if it were timed to coincide with the vibrations of Venus. Likewise, you would greatly reinforce a personal success spell by doing it on a Sunday and taking advantage of solar energy.

In addition to timing, try to include some planetary symbolism in your magickal rite. Want to give that protection spell a big boost? Plan to do your spell on a Saturday night. Use three black candles and patchouli incense, and include three pieces of jet in the work. If time permits, make a black bag in the shape of bat to carry your protection symbols in. The more refined your spells are, the better, and faster, they will work.

POPPET

A poppet is a doll fashioned from cloth or clay to represent a person or persons at whom a spell is directed. The cloth doll is usually stuffed with Spanish moss, to give it form, and herbs that correspond with the primary intention of the spell. When clay is used, small amounts of the primary herbs are crushed and then mixed in with the soft clay. Photographs, hair, nail clippings, and clothing belonging to the person are then added to the doll. The intention is to make the doll resemble the person, so that what is done to the doll will in turn actually happen to the person.

In most cases, poppets are used for love-drawing spells, healing rites, and in some cases to protect an individual from harm. The entire process is based on the first principle of magick, the Law of Similarity (also referred to as homeopathic or imitative magick), which basically states that like produces like, or that an effect may resemble its cause. Simply put, whatever you do to the symbolic representation of a person, place or thing will directly affect that same person, place, or thing.

Love-Binding Spell

The intention of this spell is to bind two people together. The first thing you need to do is make two poppets from red cloth. Leave one end of each poppet open for stuffing. Fill each poppet with equal amounts of the following ground herbs: clove, orris root, blessed thistle, coriander, yarrow, and Solomon's seal. Insert into each poppet some hair, nail clippings, and handwriting from each person. Sew up the openings. If you have facial photographs, paste these on the front side of the dolls' heads. Dress each poppet in a piece of clothing belonging to the person the poppet is to represent. The poppets are then ready to bind together using the following rite.

> *Items needed*: 3' length of red silk cord, love-drawing oil, love-drawing incense, and one red candle that will burn for at least seven hours.

Begin this spell on a Monday during the waxing moon. Place the red candle in the center of your altar and light the incense. Use a pin or sharp knife to etch the names of each person into the candle. Dress the candle with the love-drawing oil as you chant:

Candle of love, work me this spell,
That the one I do love will love me as well.

Light the candle. Pass each poppet through the smoke of the incense and then through the candle flame as you say:

Air and fire, bring forth my desire.

Place the poppet that represents you seven inches to the left side of the candle and the poppet that represents your loved one seven inches to the right of the candle. See in your mind's eye the one you love as you chant the following seven times:

I enchant you by earth and heaven
Turn to me, turn to me, turn to me by seven.
Through moonlight and the black of night
All of my love you shall requite.

[Insert name] think of me with loving pleasure
As you turn to me by daily measure.
Now turn to me, turn to me
For this I will, So Mote It Be.

Let the candle burn for one hour. Repeat the spell exactly as you have just done it for six consecutive nights. Each time you do the spell, move the poppets one inch closer to the candle. On the seventh night the dolls should be touching the candle, but not to the point that they will catch fire. At this time you will allow the candle to burn out. As soon as the candle has extinguished itself, use the red cord to bind the poppets together face to face. Conceal the dolls in a place where you and your loved one will meet.

Personal Success Poppet

This poppet will help you land a new job, get a promotion, or achieve that special goal. You will need to make a doll out of a piece of your clothing. Coarsely grind equal amounts of the following herbs: cinnamon, bay, marigold, orange peel, rosemary, witch hazel. Fill the poppet with the herb mixture and sew up the opening. Affix a full length photograph of yourself to the front of the poppet. Tie a bright yellow silk sash around the poppet. Be sure the poppet is well-made and pleasing to look at. Place the poppet in the center of your altar and consecrate it for personal success.

Items needed: One yellow or gold candle, success incense, and a shadow box large enough to hold the poppet and 60 small items.

Start this rite on a Sunday morning during the waxing moon. Light the candle and incense. Pass the poppet through the incense smoke and then the candle flame chanting six times:

With air and smoke, flame and fire
I now consecrate thee to my desire.

Hold the poppet close to your mouth. Speaking softly and with great intent, breathe your desire into the poppet. Repeat the process six times, each time passing the poppet through the incense and the flame of the candle as you repeat the chant. Allow the candle to burn for one hour.

Each day for the next 59 days, light the candle and speak of your desire. Then place an object that represents your desire next to the poppet in the box.

For example, if you wanted a pay raise, place a picture of your boss in the box next to the poppet. The next day, place some of his or her handwriting in the box, then a copy of a paycheck with your new salary on it, and so on.

At the end of the last day, allow the candle to burn out. Arrange all the items in the box along with the poppet in a manner that portrays your desire. Hang the shadow box on the wall near your desk, altar, or bed.

THE HEALING POPPET

Fashion small sticks of applewood into a human frame and cover with green cotton cloth to form the poppet. Fill with the following coarsely ground herbs: angelica, eucalyptus, ginseng, life everlasting, peppermint, spearmint, and wintergreen. Attach a photograph of the person to be healed to the poppet.

Begin the spell during the waning moon. Place the poppet on your altar next to a black candle. Using your athame, inscribe the person's name into the candle along with their ailment. Light the candle. Hold the poppet in front of the candle and chant the following seven times:

> *I take away hurt, I take away pain*
> *From you body, this illness I drain.*

Visualize the illness leaving the poppet (and therefore the body of the sick person), and flowing into the black candle. Let the candle burn out. Place the poppet in a safe place and bury the candle far from your home.

POTION

You just can't help associating glowing cauldrons and magickal potions with Witchcraft. Cartoons, movies, and fairy tales are filled with enchanting sorceresses whispering over steaming philters of fascination. One drink, and you are forever under her spell. Or, in a less favorable light, there is always a haggard old crone bending over her bubbling brew of noxious goo, intended to bring instant death to the beautiful princess.

From the *Holy Bible* to Shakespeare's *Macbeth*, we find Witches and their magick potions healing the sick and dealing out death to the enemy. According to some ancient grimoires, with the right magickal potion you can become invisible, fly on a broomstick, be forever young and beautiful, or turn your neighbor into a toad. (I like that one, and I'm sorry to say that it isn't available at this time. In fact, it may be that the powers of our ancestors have been slightly exaggerated.)

The *American Heritage Dictionary* defines the word potion as "a dose or drink, especially a liquid drink or poison." Basically potions are nothing more than herbs steeped in water for medicinal purposes. However, there are those occasions when a love potion is called for to rekindle a dying flame. A word of advice: Always be careful when making a potion. Follow the recipe exactly, and don't get creative. There are some areas of magick that need to be approached with caution, and this is one of them.

LOVE-DRAWING POTION

Items needed: One glass sauce pan, dove's blood ink, a small paint brush, sweet red wine, a metal tea ball, one cup honey, and the following herbs: 3 fresh mint leaves, 7 rosebud petals, 1 pinch orange zest (orange peel), 1 pinch coriander, and 1 pinch basil.

Put the herbs into the tea ball and set aside. On the outside of the glass pan, write the name of the person you desire seven times. On the inside of the pan, inscribe the symbol for Venus.

Fill the pan with two cups of spring water. Bring the water to a boil, insert the tea ball, turn off the heat, and allow the brew to steep for 10 minutes. Remove the tea ball and add the honey. Bring the liquid back to a boil and then reduce to a simmer. When the liquid has turned into a thick, yellow syrup, turn off the heat and allow it to cool. Pour the syrup into a bottle and label. Add several drops of the syrup to the wine, juice, or food you plan to serve your loved one.

If you are feeling brave, invite your loved one to join you in a candlelight supper. Arrange a centerpiece of red, white, and gold heart shaped candles anointed with love-drawing oil, and small vases of pink rose buds. Burn love-drawing incense and wear your most alluring outfit.

Sample Menu

White fruity wine *(add 3 drops love potion).*

Hearts of palm arranged on a bed of romaine lettuce topped with seven cocktail shrimp, served with honey mustard dressing *(add 3 drops of love potion to dressing).*

Baked quail (one each) garnished with spiced apple rings.

Asparagus with hollandaise sauce *(add 3 drops love potion to sauce).*

Long grain and wild rice with mushrooms.

Heart shaped crepes filled with fresh strawberries, topped with whipped cream *(add 3 drops love potion),* and garnished with fresh mint leaves.

Warm brandy *(add 3 drops love potion).*

RUNES

The word "rune" comes from the Old Norse *run,* which means secret. The runes were an ancient Germanic alphabet, once used for everyday communication as well as for mystical purposes and divination. The Vikings used runes to protect their homes and add power to their swords and shields. The Shamans of Scandinavia used them in healing, to cast spells, and to protect burial mounds.

The runes consist of 24 letters and one blank. The 24 runes are dedicated to three Norse deities and are divided into three sets of eight, known as *Freyr's Aett, Hagal's Aett,* and *Tyr's Aett.* The 25th, or blank, rune is called *wyrd* and symbolizes the unknowable or destiny. The traditional meaning of the blank rune is, "*In the lap of the Gods*," or "*What will, be will be.*"

Professionally crafted rune sets can be purchased at almost any New Age or Occult book store. These are nice because they come with an instruction book and storage pouch. However, it is just as easy to make your own, and infuse them with your energy during the process.

Flat, evenly shaped stones, ceramic tiles, wooden sticks, or self-hardening clay all make wonderful runes. Once they are painted or engraved with the appropriate rune symbol they become just as magickal as any store bought item. If you choose to make a set of runes you will also need to make a cloth pouch to keep them in. Choose a soft, heavy fabric in a color that will both protect and energize your runes when not in use.

Rune Stone Meanings

Freyr s Aett (first eight runes)

1. Wunjo

Joy. Joy and happiness coming into your life. Success. Good news. Joy in one's work. Affection from a loved one.
Reversed (the symbol is seen upside down): Opposite of the above.

2. Gebo

Partnership. There could be a gift involved. Always a positive sign because there is no reverse involved. Important development in a romantic relationship. Could mean marriage or business partnership.
Reversed: There is no reverse. Same as above.

3. Kano

Open. Friendly, open, and warm. Strength, energy, and power. Positive action. Problems and troubles solved easily. Good things coming into your life. Good time to start something new.

Reversed: Opposite of the above.

4. Raido

Journey. Travel with pleasure, without problems. Possible journey of the soul. Period of logical thought. A good time to buy or sell.

Reversed: Opposite of the above.

5. Ansuz

Signals. The spoken word or heeding advice. A time to think before speaking. Eloquence and ease. Discovery of secret ability.

Reversed: Lies, trickery, general deceit. Get a second opinion.

6. Thurisaz

Gateway. Unexpected good luck. Good health. Protection. Warns against headstrong action.

Reversed: No desire to heed the warnings about headstrong action, will press on regardless. Your luck is running out. Self-deception.

7. Uruz

Strength. Virility, good health and strong resistance. Of strong emotions. Could be recovering from ill health. Not much improvement in business matters. Could be a promotion.

Reversed: Imminent failure. Weak will. Low vitality. Could be a small illness.

8. Fehu

Possessions. Signifies material gain, could mean wealth. Goals are now within your grasp. Ability to overcome opposition.

Reversed: Loss or disappointment. Frustration.

Hagal s Aett (second eight runes)

9. Sowelu

Wholeness. Progress and success. Possible travel. Success with examinations. Good health. Recovery from illness. Conquest, victory and power.

Reversed: Warning against overworking. Be more considerate of your loved ones.

10. Algiz

Protection. Unexpected help from an unsympathetic person when it is most needed. A time to stand your ground. Be careful to hold tight to your principles. Invincibility.

Reversed: Vulnerability. Possible loss or injustice.

11. Perth

Initiation. Secrets. Psychic powers. An unforeseen turn of events. Possible news from afar. A joyful reunion with someone from the past.
Reversed: Disappointment.

12. Eithwaz

Defense. Try to look ahead, anticipate what is coming. A time of difficulty that will require tact and diplomacy. After a slight delay, things will improve.

Reversed: Warning, be ever watchful.

13. Jera

Harvest. You will reap the benefits of your efforts. A time to receive what has been well earned. A good time to finalize a contract or complete a task. Financial matters will improve in the days to come.

Reversed: Slight delay in financial improvement, could be a slight disappointment.

14. Isa

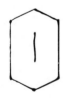

Standstill. The ice rune. Indicates that you should remain still. You may be on thin ice so it is best not to move. Time of patience and understanding. Temporary parting. Sacrifice. Submission.

Reversed: The ice is beginning to thaw, things will improve.

15. Naurthiz

Constraint. A bad time to embark on any new venture. Avoid anything that seems to be a bargain or a quick way of making money without effort. Now is the time for patience and planning.

Reversed: A time for caution. Think before acting. Make no moves at this time. If you have made an unwise choice, cut your losses and call it a day.

16. Hagalaz

Disruption. Unforeseen forces are working against you, be careful. Be prepared for an unpleasant surprise. Use caution.

Reverse: You will be able to ride this one out. Keep fighting and don't loose focus.

Tyr s Aett (third eight runes)

17. Othila

Separation. Separation in the sense of moving in a new direction at this time. There could be an inheritance or business deal on the horizon. The future is changing.

Reversed: There could be financial disputes or opposition to a plan.

18. Dagaz

Breakthrough. A time of transformation. Freedom. A weight has been lifted from your shoulders. Winning, even when the odds are stacked against you. Positive changes are coming.

Reversed: At last you can see the light at the end of the tunnel. Changes may be slow, but they're still coming.

19. Inguz

Fertility. A goal realized. A problem solved. Time to relish in the victory of a job well done. Take a rest and reflect.

Reversed: There is no reverse. Same as above.

20. Laguz

Flow. A long journey may be in the offing. A trip overseas. Time to go with the flow, your instincts. Feel rather than think.

Reversed: Heed good advice from others. Look out for temptation. Not a good sign.

21. Mannaz

Self. Time to think about yourself. Plan changes. A good time to change employment or residence. You are making steady progress.

Reversed: Keep your emotions in control at this time; changes may be postponed.

22. Ehwaz

Movement. New beginnings. A time of excitement. Change is in the air. Travel. A good time to keep things in perspective. You feel confident.

Reversed: Be mindful of others and keep emotions in check.

23. Berkana

Growth. New energies are present. New ventures are on the horizon. Could mean birth or pregnancy for a woman. New and fresh ideas. Possible sign of marriage. A favorable time.

Reversed: Keep a keen eye out for family problems, disruptions with friends, or anxiety.

24. Teiwaz

Warrior. A time to move forward and experience an adventure. New things on the horizon. A time to be bold and courageous. Victory can be yours. A time of great passion.

Reversed: There could be a loss in business. Stagnation. A time of raw emotions. Take care and be careful.

25. The last rune,
the blank rune.

 Wyrd: The unknowable. Fate. This rune tells you to place your fate with the Gods. There is nothing you can do at this time. Fate is power. You must let be what will be. Your problem or situation is way beyond your control at this time. "In the lap of the gods" signifies powerful changes, changes that are out of your control. There is no reverse for this rune. Use the other runes in your reading for advice.

RUNE LAYOUT PATTERNS

One rune method

This is by far the easiest method for reading the runes, especially if you have a specific question that needs immediate attention. Cup the runes in your hand, concentrate on your question, and ask it aloud. Place the runes back in their pouch and mix them thoroughly. Dip into the pouch and pull one rune only. This will be the answer to your question.

The nice thing about the runes, and this particular method, is that you can use them anywhere. So if you are at work and having a problem with someone or something, use your break time to consult the runes. They will provide you with a quick solution to set things right again.

Three rune method

This method is very much like the first. Cup the runes in your hand, concentrate on your question, and ask it aloud. Place the runes back in the pouch and mix them thoroughly. Pull three runes from the pouch and place them in front of you (see diagram). The first rune, to the left, indicates the basis of the problem, or present situation. The middle rune shows the vibrations currently surrounding you. The last rune, the one you placed to the right, gives you the answer or suggests the proper action to be taken.

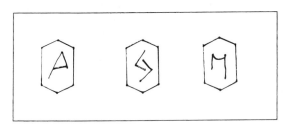

The runic cross method

Cup the runes in your hand, concentrate on your question, and speak it aloud. Put the runes back in the pouch and mix them thoroughly. Pull five runes from the pouch, one at a time. Lay the first three out in a row from left to right. The fourth goes above the center stone and the fifth is placed below the center stone. All five stones should be face down.

Turn the center stone up. This represents the present situation and what is going on now. The stone to the left is the past. Turn this stone over next; it will tell you which past vibrations are still affecting the present situation.

The top stone is next. This stone explains what outside help or self-help is necessary to improve the situation as it stands. The bottom stone is now turned over. This stone will tell you what changes can or cannot be expected.

The last stone to be turned over is the one on the right arm of the cross. This stone represents the future, the final outcome of the reading. For more clarification, pull a sixth rune. This rune is placed at the bottom of the cross, under the fifth stone. This sixth rune will denote new, fresh influences that could affect the situation and its final outcome.

If you are new to Witchcraft and uncertain about which method of divination to choose, start with the runes. They are easy to make and convenient to use, and there is very little left up to personal interpretation. Because of their size, runes travel well. They can be read almost anywhere and in any situation. Keep a set of runes in your purse, briefcase, or school locker. Use your coffee break, lunch hour, or recess time to consult them about the events of the day.

The best way to become proficient with the runes, or any of the divination systems mentioned, is by using them on a regular basis. Before you leave for work or start your day, take a moment to consult your runes, cards, or tea leaves. You don't need to be in crisis to seek higher wisdom or spiritual guidance. Use your divination skills to help set daily and weekly goals or to indicate areas where personal progress can be made. A simple question like "What should I work on today?" will provide you with the motivation and direction needed to live the magickal life.

Shamanism

Shamanism is probably the oldest magickal system in the world and probably comes from Siberia and Central Asia. Its practices include the use of visions, altered states of consciousness, and contact with nature gods and spirits. Evidence of Shamanism can be seen almost everywhere; the most often cited examples are found in the cave paintings in southern France. These paintings date back to 35,000 B.C. and depict men dressed in animal skins performing a hunting ritual. Through imitation and participation with the animals and the natural world, the Shaman obtained his or her empowerment.

When our Paleolithic ancestors came to North America from Siberia, they brought magickal practices with them. As these groups sprea across the continent, different cultures, folkways, and belief systems developed among the tribes.

The practices and rites of the Shamans were geared to the tribe's cultural orientation. The Shaman of a hunting tribe would usually work with the spirits of animals; the Shaman of a tribe involved with agriculture would work with the elements that supported a good harvest. All considered the changing of the seasons as well as birth, death, marriage, and puberty to be of importance and addressed these occasions according to tribal custom.

Originally the Shaman was a member of the tribe, who, through trance, journeyed to other worlds. While the Shaman was in this altered state, he would commune with spirits, gain wisdom, and acquire new methods of healing. The prime purpose of the Shaman was to bring back information from his journey to help guide and protect his people.

THE VISION QUEST

The Shaman is a trained individual who enters and leaves states of consciousness at will. While in these states of altered consciousness, he or she will journey to various domains of the inner world. This journey that the Shaman undertakes usually puts him or her in contact with spirits of ancestors, totem animals, and higher plane teachers. The purpose of the journey is to obtain power, knowledge, and wisdom from the inner world contacts and bring it back to the realm of reality.

Also included in the journey process is the custom of going on a vision quest. In the traditional vision quest, the individual is sent off into seclusion, without food, and with only a blanket for warmth, to "catch a spirit." During this time of separation from the world of reality, the person acquires his or her guardian spirit and a portion of his or her medicine power.

Medicine Power

The term medicine refers to an individual's unique talents and skills and the ability to blend these skills or talents with the forces of nature. When skills are combined with the knowledge and wisdom gained from an inner world journey or vision quest, they become the medicine power used to heal and help others.

Places, personal objects, fetishes, and animals are also considered to have medicine power. When the Shaman goes into a trance, he or she searches for the special power of a place, object, or spirit. Once the answer to the question, problem, or situation has been acquired, the Shaman will then return to the world of reality, bringing the healing answer with him or her.

Cleansing and Smudging

Before every ceremony or healing, the individuals participating should be cleansed of bad feelings and negative vibrations that may be attached to them. The cleansing is accomplished by passing smoke from burning herbs over the body. The most commonly used herbs are sage (to drive out unwanted spirits), cedar (to carry prayers to the creator), and sweetgrass (to bring in good spirits and influences).

Another form of purification (considered to be the best) is the sweat lodge. During the rite of the sweat lodge all the powers of the universe—earth, water, fire, air, breath, and sky—are called upon. The lodge is built from red willows and covered with hides. In the center of the lodge is a pit into which heated rocks, called the stone people, are placed. As each stone is placed in the pit, it is named and receives a force or power of nature. During the sweat lodge, the sacred pipe and the smudge are used with prayers to cleanse and purify those taking part in the ceremony.

THE SACRED PIPE

The sacred prayer pipe is the "tool of tools," the most powerful and most cherished gift of Native American tribes. The prayers and desires of the tribe are carried to the Great Spirit and Sky Father on the smoke from the pipe. The pipe is used in all Native American ceremonies and is considered to be the axis mundi, the central point of time and space, the supreme support of all things, and that which connects heaven and Earth. The pipe acts as a traveling altar and becomes the center of focus for all rituals or ceremonies.

The pipe's bowl represents the Goddess and Earth Mother aspect of the Great Spirit. The pipe's stem is the God and Sky Father part of the Great Spirit. When these two elements are united for the purpose of sharing breath, they create peace, harmony, and unity among those participating in the ceremony.

THE MEDICINE WHEEL

The medicine wheel is a symbol of the universe and represents completion. It is a place where men and women learn to sing the song of the world, become whole again, and unite with the Earth Mother and Sky Father. When properly constructed, the medicine wheel becomes transition, self-realization, and communication with the spirits of nature.

The wheel is constructed by clearing an area large enough to accommodate the people using in it. A stone or stake driven into the ground to symbolize the Great Spirit marks the center of the wheel. Stakes or rocks painted in the corresponding elemental colors mark the four cardinal points. Other rocks, sticks, sacred objects, flowers, and feathers are used to designate certain areas. Simple or elaborate, the medicine wheel serves as a place for meditation, a symbol of the universe, or a circle of protection for sacred ceremonies.

The Guardian Spirit

The Shaman believes that everyone is born with a guardian spirit. This belief is common among a lot of different peoples, especially those practicing nature oriented religions. During initiations, vision quests, and trances, the individual is able to communicate with his or her guardian spirit. In some societies it is believed that this guardian spirit is in part related to the spirit of the individual, a sort of eternal cosmic twin energy.

The totem spirit serves in different capacities. It can be a badge or emblem of a tribe or clan, representing their principal purpose or focus. The totem can also serve as a sacred personal talisman chosen for symbolism pertinent to the individual's personality. In either case, it usually provides protection, gives counsel during times of trouble, and when properly appeased brings prosperity.

Sun

Symbolically, the sun represents supreme masculine power, omniscient divinity, heart of the cosmos, and splendor of the universe. In most traditions the sun is the universal father, with the moon as the mother. Constantly rising and setting, the sun symbolizes both life and death, and the renewal of life through death. The sun is the visible image of divine goodness.

Talisman

According to MacGregor Mathers, ceremonial magician, author, and founder of the Golden Dawn magickal order, a talisman is "a magickal figure charged with the force it is intended to represent," and is usually constructed to attain a particular result. When it is properly constructed, a talisman's effectiveness is obvious immediately, or at least within seven days of its construction. Generally talismans are employed for use in obtaining long-term goals. For example, a talisman might be constructed to get a job promotion, to induce love that will lead to marriage, or to create a barrier of protection around a home or loved one.

The nice thing about a talisman is that once it has been created and charged, it can be left to do its work; the energy set up by the operator continues to work over a set period of time. Talismans work like batteries and have the benefit of being self-recharging to some extent (provided they've been properly constructed). This recharging ability is due to the relationship between the talisman and a corresponding symbolic force.

Talismans play an important role in magick, because they have the ability to summon and hold elemental energies and powers. Most importantly, they allow you to intensify and extend your personal magnetism beyond the normal ranges. This is made possible because of the occult symbolism that is embodied within the talisman.

Ancient magickal seals, like those found in the Key of Solomon, contain power that has been built up over hundreds of years of use. The symbolism within these seals reflects the inner universe of human nature and provides a means by which it can be manipulated and controlled.

Talismans have the ability to unlock the powers within us and to provide access to the powers outside of us. As a carefully crafted vehicle of magickal force, the talisman directs energy toward a desired goal to help bring it into reality. The most widely recognized seals or talismans come from the Key of Solomon. They correspond to the seven major planets and can be used alone or added to spells. Their presence within a magickal work aligns that work with the planetary energy being represented.

Talisman Seals from The Key of Solomon

The first pentacle of the sun. The countenance of El Shaddai, favored by those who wish to obtain all things that they desire. Incorporate this talisman into magical works designed to bring success and prosperity.

The fourth pentacle of the sun. Designed to enable the owner to see others as they really are. When this seal is in the vicinity of a friend or foe, their true thoughts will be revealed. It also enables the owner to see spirits. Use to uncover the truth in all situations.

The first pentacle of the moon. Said to call forth the spirits of the moon to open all doors, no matter how they may be fastened. Use this talisman to help gain entrance into clubs, sororities, and magical lodges. Can help with intuition and psychic work.

 The fourth pentacle of the moon. Will serve to defend its owner from evil and from all injury to the body or soul. It also gives the knowledge and virtue of all herbs and stones to whoever possesses it. Combine this talisman with a protection spell.

 The first pentacle of Mars. Said to invoke the powers of Mars for gaining courage, enthusiasm, ambition, and all physical accomplishments. Use in personal power rituals to boost strength, endurance, and magnetism.

 The fourth pentacle of Mars. Use to bring victory in war, to lend its power to bring victory over all enemies, and to vindicate its owner in all situations. Combine this pentacle with protection rituals and spells, as well as those to overcome obstacles.

The third pentacle of Mercury. Is used to influence the written word, tending to make one eloquent in letters, papers, or any form of writing. Because Mercury is the planet of communication, this is a great talisman to use when trying to sell your ideas to another by way of the written word.

The fourth talisman of Mercury. Will help its owner acquire knowledge and understanding of all things. Can be used to penetrate hidden thoughts. A great talisman to use if you are in school or studying for a test. Can also help you learn what others may be thinking.

 The fourth pentacle of Jupiter. Used to acquire great wealth, riches, and honor. It should be engraved on silver and used to enhance prosperity and money-drawing rituals or spells. Will bring honor as well as wealth to its owner.

 The sixth pentacle of Jupiter. Will protect its owner from all earthly dangers. By simply regarding the talisman every day and repeating " thou shalt never perish," one is surrounded by the protective force of the talisman. Can be used in conjunction with protection spells and rituals.

 The second pentacle of Venus. Is used for obtaining grave honor, and accomplishing all desires in matters of the heart. This pentacle belongs to Venus and will bring its owner honor in all things, especially those which involve love. Add this pentacle to love and friendship spells.

The fourth pentacle of Venus. Has great power and will to compel the spirits of Venus to obey. When used with love spells, this talisman will force any person you wish to come to you. Pentacle should be engraved on copper.

 The second pentacle of Saturn. Of great value when meeting with adversaries in business. This talisman should be carried when looking for work or when negotiating financial deals. Use in combination with the fourth pentacle of Jupiter to protect monetary gain.

 The fifth pentacle of Saturn. Defends those who invoke the spirits of Saturn during the night, chasing away bad spirits and guarding treasure. It is a good talisman to use to protect the home and all the items in it. Place on the back of a mirror to reflect negative vibrations.

(For a comprehensive listing of all the planetary pentacles and related talismans see *The Key of Solomon The King* (Clavicula Salomonis), translated from ancient manuscripts in the British Museum by S. Liddell MacGregor Mathers and then prepared for publication under the editorship of L.W. de Laurence around 1900. Since then, *The Key of Solomon The King* has been reprinted on a regular basis by various British and American publishers. The most recent issue comes from Samuel Weiser, Inc., 1974, with a forward by Richard Cavendish.)

TRIPLE GODDESS

The triple Goddess can be found in almost all mythologies. She was at once virgin, mother, and crone; the waxing, full, and waning moon. All that was feminine, enchanting, ripe, and wise. One of the most popular triple goddesses was the Greek Hecate, who reigned over heaven, earth, and the underworld, where she controlled birth, life, and death.

To demonstrate her triple nature, Hecate carried three magick symbols, the key, rope, and dagger. The key unlocked the door to the underworld—opening the way to the mysteries and secrets of knowledge and the afterlife. The rope symbolized the umbilical cord of rebirth and renewal—the connection between humanity and the Goddess. The double edged dagger symbolised her power to cut through delusion.

Hecate was the giver of visions, magick, and regeneration, the guardian at the gates of the underworld. As a guardian, she was associated with crossroads and the ability to see beyond death. This is because when you stand at a crossroads, you can view the past from whence you came, as well as the future, your destination.

INVOCATION OF HECATE

(To ask for Hecate's blessing or help)

> *Items needed*: One large black candle, censer, church charcoal, Hecate incense (three oz. black incense base mixed with one pinch patchouli leaves, one tsp. granulated myrrh, three drops patchouli oil, and three drops jasmine oil), black cloth, altar, chalice of red wine, plate of moon cakes (sugar cookies cut into crescent moons), piece of rope, old fashioned door key, and your athame.

For optimum effectiveness, perform this invocation at a crossroads and as near to midnight as possible. Before the ritual inscribe your name and desire on the black candle. Gather together all the items called for, along with something to serve as an altar, and proceed to the crossroads. Set the altar on top of the crossroads, where all four paths meet.

Arrange the altar with the black candle in the center; the athame front center, the rope right center, the key left center, and the censer center back. Light the charcoal and some incense. Take several deep breaths. Relax. Focus on your desire. When you feel the time is right, light the black candle, pick up the wine and hold it in offering as you invoke Hecate.

> Thou who whispers, gentle and strong,
> Thou for whom my soul doth long,
> By most men you are seldom seen
> You are the virgin, mother, and queen.
> Through the veil you pass with pride,
> I beckon thee now to be at my side,
> Hecate.
>
> Thou who knows, thou who conceals
> Thou who gives birth, thou who feels,
> For you are the Goddess and mother of all
> Pray thee now— come as I call.
> Now through the mist I hear your voice,
> I invoke the gracious goddess by choice,
> Hecate.
>
> Thou who suffers as all men die
> Doth with her victim in love lie.
> You are the goddess and crone of despair
> And with you our ending we must share.
> I feel thy passion, I feel thy presence,
> I rapture in your vital essence,
> Hecate.

I pray thee dancer of eternal bliss,
Bestow upon me thy wondrous kiss,
Let now thy light, love, and power
Become as one with me this hour.
For you are the creatress of heaven and Earth
So to my dreams and wishes give birth,
Hecate.

Ask for your desire and Hecate's blessing. Drink some of the wine and eat one of the cakes in her honor. Allow the candle to burn for one hour and then extinguish it. Leave a libation of wine and the rest of the cakes on the crossroads. Pack up all your magickal items and leave the area as you found it.

UNCROSSING

Uncrossing is used in Witchcraft and magick to remove evil influences, negative spells, and black magick. For the most part, an uncrossing ritual is done during the waning moon or during the dark moon, the few hours before the moon begins to wax. In some cases the energy will be sent directly back to the individual who sent it in the first place. However, sometimes this is not possible. If the identity of the individual is not known, or if the exact specifications of the original crossing ritual cannot be determined, then the energy is magickally eliminated, usually by forcing it into a proper receptacle that can be buried or burned.

UNCROSSING RITUAL

Items needed: One black candle, salt, fireproof pot, black cord, and 150 proof alcohol or Florida water.

One hour before the moon begins to wax, when it's at its darkest, set your altar with the necessary items. Cast your magick circle with the salt. Tie the black cord around the waist of the person on whom a negative spell has been placed and stand them in the center of the circle. Light the black candle and say with great force:

> Fast as the wind, swift as the night,
> Banish the evil with the light.
> Seek thee out where ere thee be
> And invoke the law of three.

Light the firepot. Then, as you would do with smudge, stand arms' length away and run the firepot up and down in front of the person. Still holding the pot, walk three times around the person, chanting:

> I end your curses with power of thought,
> All your works have come to naught.
> Be gone, be gone, all evil rebound,
> Then perish and fade into the ground.
> As fire and flame, pure cleansing light
> Banish forever [insert name]'s plight.

Place the firepot on the altar. Untie the black cord and allow it to fall to the ground, still within the salt circle. Have the person step out of the circle. Place the still burning firepot on top of the spot were the person was standing. While the pot burns, both chant:

> Thou who caused this torment bad,
> Shall live a life woeful and sad.

When the pot has completely burned out, extinguish the candle. Dig a small hole in the center of the salt circle and bury the cord and black candle. Cover with dirt. Pack up all your tools, turn, and walk away. Do not look back.

Unicorn

The Unicorn is a mythical beast with one phallic horn on its forehead, a horselike body, and a goat's beard. It symbolizes the union of opposites, undivided sovereign power, virginity, and love.

As a water conner, the horn of the unicorn can detect poison in water and render it harmless. In Christian symbolism, the horn of the unicorn denotes Christ and the Father as one, and as an antidote to poison, it represents the power of Christ to destroy sin.

Most Wiccans view the unicorn as a magickal beast that has the power to enchant virgins and beautiful women. When crushed and powdered, his horn makes a powerful aphrodisiac. It is believed that Morgan la Fey used the powder to seduce King Arthur and bear his child.

Unicorn Enchantment

Items needed: One white candle, gold paint, fairy dust, and a photograph of the person to be enchanted. On one side of the candle, paint the silhouette of the unicorn, and write the name of your beloved next to it. Place the candle on top of the photograph and light it. Sprinkle some of the fairy dust over the flame and photo as you chant:

By unicorns, fairies, and mystical dust,
Now for me does [insert name] lust.
His [her] passion burns as does this fire
With aching torment and desire.

Allow the candle to burn out. Place the photo under your pillow, sprinkle with fairy dust, and dream of your loved one. He or she should be yours in seven days.

VISUALIZATION

Creative visualization is a technique Witches and magicians use to make their dreams come true. In essence, it is a fancy name for the old children's game of "let's pretend." The idea is to create an image in your mind's eye of something you desire. You then empower this image through concentrated meditation, forcing the image into reality. If you want something bad enough and think about it hard enough, it will happen.

The keys to making creative visualization work are best expressed in the witch's mystical triangle.

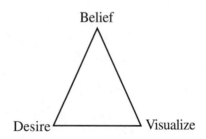

Belief: The number one key is the most important. The more your believe in your goal or object of desire, the more likely you are to achieve it. What you believe can happen, you can make happen.

Desire: You must have a powerful desire. This means you must be totally, passionately, and thoroughly engrossed with your desire. It must be so strong that it will take precedence over all other things. You must be obsessed with your goal so as to stir the emotions into action.

Visualize: For creative visualization to work, you must be able to create a clear mental picture of your desire. You must be able to create in your mind's eye an exact image of what you want, as if you were looking at a photograph of it. To make creative visualization work, you have to create a mental picture so strong that the sheer power of your will forces it to manifest

The key to magick lies in your ability to visualize your desire into reality. There can be no doubt, lack of desire, or impotent emotion involved. Every ounce of energy and power you have must be put into your visualization if you want it to manifest. This means you must focus your attention and psychic energy with laser-sharp accuracy toward the object of your desire. Then you must believe that what you are doing will really happen.

WAND

In practice, the wand is the primary working tool of the Witch. It represents his or her rod of power and authority. During ritual, the wand becomes an extension of the Witch's magickal jurisdiction. Personal power is forced through the wand, with a laser-like intensity, toward a specific target. When the psychic energy and target meet, activation occurs, and the Witch's intentions are set into motion.

The wand, like every magickal tool, has a distinctive character and represents a specific action, thought, or emotion. In Witchcraft, the wand is associated with the element of Air, which is symbolic of the mind, the intellect, and communication. It provides the Witch with a means of channeling abstract thought forms, as well as energy, onto the material plane. Once the thought form takes shape and is energized, it will become the medium to manifest desire.

The main reason the wand is so popular is its simplicity. There is nothing complicated or difficult to understand about its construction or purpose. The wand is simply a tool for channeling energy from the spiritual plane to the material plane.

A wand is very easy to make. A small branch with a crystal or favorite rock attached, wrapped in leather, works nicely. A simple copper tube with crystals, amethyst, or rose quartz connected to the ends produces a wonderful energy conductor. Brass tubing found in most craft shops has all sorts of possibilities, and even wooden dowels from a lumber store can, with some imagination, be turned into elegant wands.

My wand is made from copper tubing, is 11″ long, and has a rose quartz on one end and an amethyst on the other. Connecting the ends is silver solder spiraled down the shaft. On this there are four stones: garnet, rhodochrosite, gem silica, and lapis. Because of the magickal properties associated with these particular gems, this combination helps to balance power through self-love and spiritual insight.

WAND CONSECRATION

Items needed: One white candle, bowl of salt, bowl of water, sandalwood incense, wand.

Perform this rite during the waxing moon. Light the white candle and the sandalwood incense as you say:

Let now the powers of life and light
Bless and protect me on this night.

Pick up the wand and sprinkle it with salt, pass it through the incense smoke and candle flame and then sprinkle with water as you say:

Forces of good, of life and of light,
Descend into my wand this night
For this is a tool of my sacred art
So your powers I ask, now impart.
With the elements of Earth, Air, Fire, and Sea,
I now baptize, bless, and consecrate thee!
My will be done, So Mote It Be.

WATER

Water has long been seen as the source of all potentialities in existence. It is associated with the Great Mother, the universal womb, birth, and fertility. Water is emblematic of the life-giving and life-destroying capabilities of the cosmos. As an element, it encourages moderation and cools anger brought on by too much Fire. It also stabilizes the illusions caused by an excess of Air.

WATER MAGICK

Water Condenser

A water condenser is a special, magickally charged, potion. It is made from herbs, water, and alcohol, to which a bit of gold or silver is added. The condenser helps to intensify and store the powers from the herbs and metal for future magickal use.

The water condenser are good for attracting love, friendships, affection, good health and emotional stability.

Water Correspondence Chart

VALUES	Emotion, intuition, devotion, mysticism
COLORS	Green, turquoise
SYMBOLS	Crescent, shells, boats, ship wheel, anchor, cup
TOOLS	Vessel, grail, chalice, cauldron
PLANTS	Aloe, cucumber, dulse, gardenia, lily, lotus, willow
STONES	Aquamarine, chrysocolla, moonstone, mother-of-pearl
PLACES	Ocean, river, lakes, ponds, waterfalls, beaches
ZODIAC	Cancer, Scorpio, Pisces
ARCHANGEL	Gabriel
TIMES	Autumn, sunset
DIRECTIONS	West
PROCESSES	Love, nurture, sensitivity, psychic ability, healing

Love Drawing Condenser

Items Needed: Small pot or cauldron, spring water, pink or red rose petals, 8 oz. vodka, clear glass bowl, a piece of silver, plastic wrap, ruby red bottle.

Pour the water into the pot and bring to a boil. Add a handful of rose petals, cover the pot, and turn off the heat. Allow the petals to steep for one hour. Add some vodka to the mixture to preserve it.

When the mixture has cooled, pour it into a the bowl. Place the piece of silver in the bottom of the bowl. Place your hands over the bowl and infuse the condenser with your thoughts and desires as you chant:

From Earth to Water and river to sea
The love I desire shall come unto me.
By power of herb and deep emotion,
Bring true love and deep devotion.

Cover the bowl with the plastic wrap and place it in direct moonlight. Allow the condenser about an hour to absorb the power from the moon. Store the condenser in the ruby red bottle, along with the silver. Label and use in love-drawing spells or to dress candles.

Water Wishing Spell

Items needed: One large white bowl, one blue glass seven day candle, white flower petals, rosewater.

Place the candle in the center of the bowl. Fill the bowl with water and add seven drops of rosewater and the flower petals.

While stirring the water with your right index finger, speak of your desire. Light the candle and say:

Water and Fire
Manifest my desire.

Leave the bowl until the candle has completely burned out. Pour the water on a growing plant or in your garden. Affirm once more your desire.

WATER INCENSE AND FRAGRANCE

Aloes Wood *(love, strength):* Burn aloes wood to attract love and good fortune. Very high spiritual vibrations, will attract love if carried or worn.

Cherry *(love, divination):* Mix one drop cherry oil with three drops Orchid oil, and three drops violet oil, wear to attract love. Add a tiny bit of cherry oil to vanilla and myrrh crystals, burn during divination to reveal your true love.

Gardenia *(love, peace, healing):* Burn gardenia incense to create a peaceful and loving atmosphere. Use gardenia petals to attract good spirits and love.

Jasmine *(love, money, prophetic dreams):* Wear jasmine oil to attract spiritual love. Mix three drops jasmine oil with sandalwood chips and frankincense and burn for prophetic dreams.

Lilac *(protection):* Plant lilacs in window boxes or around the outside of the house for protection. Mix lilac oil with sandalwood chips and burn for protection.

Rose *(love, luck, psychic power):* Bathe with rosewater to attract love. String rose hips together to make a love-drawing necklace. Rose petals sprinkled around the bedroom and home will bring peace and harmony.

WITCH BOTTLE

The Witch bottle is most often used to protect personal property and the home. It is easy to make and very effective. All you need is a small glass jar with a tight fitting lid. You then fill the jar with bits of broken glass, nails, thorns, steel wool, nettles, vinegar, salt, and your own urine.

At midnight, during the waning of the moon, place the bottle and a black candle on your altar. Light the black candle, and completely cover the lid of the jar with the melted wax to form a permanent seal. On top of the lid, inscribe a pentagram into the wax. Hold both hands over the bottle and speak the following incantation:

Candle of black in this dark hour
Grant to me the magick power
To reverse the flow of evil cast
And leave all sorrow in the past.

Allow the candle to burn out. Bury the jar near your front door as a shield of protection. The Witch bottle should be recharged every three months in order to retain its strength.

YARROW

Yarrow grows with a straight, angular stem bearing gray-green, feathery, finely divided leaves. Referred to as "bad man's plaything," yarrow is often the main ingredient in 17th and 18th century love spells. Even today, the stalk of the herb is still used by Chinese fortunetellers as an aid in consulting the *I Ching*.

YARROW LOVE SPELL

To dream of the one you will love and marry, from a church yard pluck a stalk of yarrow on the night of the full moon saying:

> *Yarrow, sweet yarrow, that I have found,*
> *With love I pluck thee from the ground.*
> *As a man takes a woman sweet and dear*
> *In my dreams this night let my true love appear.*

Place the yarrow stalk under your pillow and you will dream of the person you will marry.

ZODIAC

The word zodiac is derived from the Greek *zoidiakos,* or "figures of animals." It resembles a circle that has been divided into 12 sections of 30 degrees each and is traversed by the sun, moon, and planets each year. Its 12 signs are named after the adjacent constellations that form a great belt around the earth. Each sign governs a month, represented by a symbolic figure that is related to one of the four Elements and human condition.

As the sun enters a sign, all persons born during that period inherit or express the qualities and traits it represents. The real significance of the zodiac concerns the process by which primordial energy passes from the potential to the virtual or from sprit to matter. When the sun, moon, and planets pass through a sign they unify the energy of that sign to complement the monthly period and complete a segment of yearly cycle.

The Zodiac Wheel of The Year

THE TWELVE SIGNS OF THE ZODIAC

Aries

March 21 through April 19. Symbol: ram; Element: Fire; Quality: cardinal; Ruling planet: Mars; Metal: iron; Gem: ruby or red jasper; Color: scarlet; Plant: geranium or sage.

Like the Ram, Aries has a reputation for egotism, action, self-assertion, and the desire to be first. Aries is a masculine sign that is looking for identity. Aries can be fearless on the outside and timid on the inside. The ram spontaneously falls in love, but usually has a difficult time verbalizing his or her feelings. Headstrong and aggressive, the Aries has tremendous power and energy. Aries are leaders, entrepreneurs, and adventurers, usually pushing the envelope in their direction.

Taurus

April 20 through May 19. Symbol: bull; Element: Earth; Quality: fixed; Ruling planet: Venus, Metal: copper; Gem: topaz or emerald; Color: red and orange; Plant: clover and mallow.

Taurus is stable, conservative, and practical, and values the comfortable, unchanging way of life. Taurus is down-to-Earth and one of the most productive signs, always searching for the true value and meaning of life. Like a bull, the Taurus usually remains passive and content, but when angered will attack. Fidelity and consistency are the sign's virtues; obstinacy and refusal to change are its weaknesses.

Gemini

May 20 through June 20. Symbol: twins; Element: Air; Quality: mutable; Ruling planet: Mercury; Metal: quicksilver; Gem: alexandrite; Color: orange; Plant: orchid and gladiolus.

The search for variety is the trademark of the Gemini, who is always thinking and looking. Maddeningly inconsistent; Geminis can argue one point of view one day, and the completely opposite view the next. The symbol that represents this sign embodies the essential split in its nature of always trying to view both sides of the coin at the same time. Geminis are the true Jacks of all trades, but unfortunately if their talents are spread too thin, they may not realize their dreams.

Cancer

June 21 through July 22. Symbol: crab; Element: Water; Quality: cardinal; Ruling planet: moon; Metal: silver; Gem: emerald or turquoise; Color: amber; Plant: lotus or comfrey.

The crab, with its soft and fleshy body covered by a hard and protective shell, depicts the nature of this sign. Cancer is the embodiment of compassion, caring, and maternal instincts, but it often hides these emotions behind a mask of indifference. When upset, Cancers withdraw into their shells but still have sharp pincers to attack with. Cancers are renowned homemakers and require domestic stability for happiness. As long as Cancers have a strong base from which to operate and to which they can retreat, they will succeed and reach their goals.

Leo

July 23 through August 21. Symbol: lion; Element: Fire; Quality: fixed; Ruling planet: sun; Metal: gold; Gem: opal or zircon; Color: yellowish green; Plant: sunflower or cyclamen.

Just like the king of the jungle, Leo is proud, ostentatious, and the most egotistical of all the signs. It takes effort for Leos not to cross the line and become excessively vain, arrogant, and selfish. Leos live to make an impression and need to have an audience. Leos can be difficult to love and to work with, as they have very little sense of anyone but themselves. If Leos can learn to accept responsibility, personal change, and the fact that others have feelings too, they make energetic and fun companions. To thrive, the Leo needs space and a spotlight.

Virgo

August 22 through September 22.
Symbol: virgin; Element: Earth;
Quality: mutable; Ruling planet:
Mercury; Metal: quicksilver; Gem:
diamond or chrysolite; Color: light green; Plant: snowdrop, lily,
and narcissus.

The Virgo is practical, productive, and prepared to sacrifice its own interests in order to complete its assigned tasks. Virgos are always searching for something meaningful to do, which is an open door for those who would take advantage of their good nature and willingness to help. This sign is the embodiment of service. However, they are often fussy and obsessed with cleanliness and order to the point that they lose their ability to be spontaneous. Virgos need to balance out their perfectionism.

Libra

September 23 through October 22.
Symbol: scales; Element: Air;
Quality: cardinal; Ruling planet:
Venus; Metal: copper; Gem: jade; Color: emerald green; Plant:
aloe.

The scales are the key to understanding Libra, who is constantly weighing the possibilities, and the choice at hand.

Often crippled by indecision, in desperation the Libra will resort to making a choice, any choice, even though it may not be the best option. Ideally Libra's function is to resolve opposing possibilities by seeking a third way. Ruled by Venus, the Libra likes things that are aesthetically pleasing, charming, and artistic. Libras tend to hide personal flaws they imagine might offend.. They are diplomats and like peaceful, harmonious surroundings.

Scorpio

October 23 through November 21. Symbol: scorpion; Element: Water; Quality: fixed; Ruling planet: Mars (with Pluto as a co-ruler); Metal: iron; Gem: carnelian; Color: greenish blue; Plant: cactus, hound's tongue.

The search for transformation is what motivates Scorpios. The intense emotions of this sign are toughened by the influence of Mars, which gives it an obsessive, sometimes abusive, quality. Those born under this sign have a keen sense for what is right and wrong. Scorpios are usually fascinated with the dark, hidden side of things. They make great Witches and magicians. The sign's greatest strength is commitment, the ability to see things through to the end. Its greatest weakness is a reluctance to change or forgive.

Sagittarius

November 22 through December 21. Symbol: archer; Element: Fire; Quality: mutable; Ruling planet: Jupiter; Metal: tin; Gem: sapphire; Color: blue; Plant: rush and pimpernel.

Sagittarius is a deep, complicated sign, a mixture of instinct and reason always searching for wisdom. The combination of mutability and fire makes this sign unstable; its plans are often dropped before completion. Often possessed by wanderlust, idealism, and the search for truth, Sagittarius needs freedom. The sign's greatest strength is optimism and enthusiasm, and its weakness is impracticality. However, when their faith is strong, Sagittarians get along well with little material success.

Capricorn

December 22 through January 20. Symbol: goat; Element: Earth;, Quality: cardinal; Ruling planet: Saturn; Metal: lead; Gem: black opal or tourmaline; Color: indigo; Plant: thistle.

The Capricorn is the ideal industrialist or merchant, letting no humanitarian concerns interfere with important business or money-making opportunities. Capricorns harbor powerful emotions that as Earth signs they find difficult to express. This sign can be very unimaginative, serious, and cautious when drawn into the world of materialism. Capricorns' greatest traits are their ability to heal and to have great visions. Their greatest downfall is being manipulative and deceitful.

Aquarius

January 21 through February 19. Symbol: water bearer; Element: Air; Quality: fixed; Ruling Planet: Saturn (with Uranus as co-ruler); Metal: lead; Gem: lapis lazuli or aquamarine; Color: violet; Plant: absinthe, fennel, and buttercup.

The search for the Holy Grail defines the essence of Aquarius. This enigmatic sign is ruled by two planets with totally incompatible natures, one desiring order, the other tearing it down. The contradictions in this sign's character are what makes it interesting. Aquarians are concerned, sometimes to the point of obsession, with being new, radical, and different. They are often eccentric, frequently awkward, and always demanding freedom. The Aquarian is best at developing new ideas but needs others to help carry them out.

Pisces

February 20 through March 20. Symbol: two fishes; Element: Water; Quality: mutable; Ruling planet: Jupiter (with Neptune as co-ruler); Metal: tin; Gem: *pearl or amethyst; Color: crimson; Plant: opium and birthwort.*

Pisces is the most unworldly of all the signs. It leans toward religion and mysticism and often withdraws from the world. Emotional and sensitive, Pisceans tend to wear many disguises to mask their vulnerability. Imaginative, artistic, and self-sacrificing, Pisces will succeed on the stage or in the church. Pisces' strength lies in its ability to rise above materialism; its weakness lies in handling the real world.

THE ZODIAC AND MAGICK

Knowledge is power, we all desire power over our own lives. No one gets into magick to save the whales or the suffering masses. You can join the peace corps to do that. You get into magick to reclaim your personal power and hopefully gain some control over your life and future.

We all wear masks to hide our imagined flaws and imperfections. So, if you know the birth signs of people you're dealing with, you have a better idea of discerning who they really are, as opposed to the images they portray. By knowing something about the individual, you avoid doing things that will offend him or her and thus create an uncomfortable situation. This type of knowledge can be of great magickal value when beginning a long-term relationship, starting partnerships, getting your business proposal on the table, as well as when you are just trying to appease your mother-in-law.

For example, to attract a Cancer (who basks in the light of domesticity), you will need to avoid any type of sudden movement that might infringe upon the home life. If you are an Aries contemplating a long-term business partnership, avoid the Leo—a space big enough for the two of you does not exist. That Geminis looking for love should steer clear of Libras, because by the time they get through analyzing the situation, they will be too old to do anything about it. And if your mother-in-law is a Scorpio, just agree with her.

Since we are all born under a specific Zodiacal sign, the energies of that sign can be incorporated into magickal rites and spells. If you are planning to do a love attraction spell, consider incorporating the Zodiac symbols of the one you desire into your rite. Use a Zodiac candle to represent your boss in that promotional spell you are planning. And, just before that big proposal, burn a Zodiac candle for each person involved, as you visualize success.

BIBLIOGRAPHY

Baer, Randall, and Vicki Baer. *Windows of Light*. San Francisco: Harper and Row, 1984.

Beyerl, Paul. *Master Book of Herbalism*. Custer, Wash.: Phoenix Publishing, 1984.

Bias, Clifford. *Ritual Book of Magic*. York Beach, Maine: Samuel Weiser, 1982.

Cunningham, Scott. *The Complete Book of Incense, Oils, and Brews*. St. Paul: Llewellyn Publications, 1989.

Drury, Nevill. *The Elements of Shamanism*. Rockport, Mass.: Element Books, 1989.

Eason, Cassandra. *The Handbook of Ancient Wisdom*. New York: Sterling Publishing, 1997.

Goodwin, Joscelyn. *Mystery Religions In The Ancient World*. San Francisco: Harper and Row, 1981.

Green, Marion. *A Witch Alone*. Wellingborough, England: The Aquarian Press, 1991.

Green, Marion. *The Elements of Natural Magic England.* Rockport, Mass.: Element Books, 1992.

Heisler, Roger. *Path To Power, It's All In Your Mind.* York Beach, Maine: Samuel Weiser, 1990.

Huson, Paul. *Mastering Witchcraft.* New York: Perigree/G. P. Putnam and Sons, 1970.

Katzeff, Paul. *Full Moons.* Secaucus, N.J.: Citadel Press, 1981.

Lewis, J. R., and E. D. Oliver. *Angels A to Z.* Detroit: Visible Ink Press, 1996.

Liddell, S., and MacGregor Mathers. *The Key of Solomon The King.* York Beach, Maine: Samuel Weiser, 1974.

Meyer, Marvin W. *The Ancient Mysteries: A Source Book.* San Francisco: Harper and Row, 1987.

Sabrina, Lady. *Cauldron of Transformation.* St. Paul: Llewellyn Publications, 1996.

Sabrina, Lady. *Reclaiming The Power: The How and Why of Practical Ritual Magic.* St. Paul: Llewellyn Publications, 1992.

Skelton, Robin. *Spell Craft.* York Beach, Maine: Samuel Weiser, 1978.

Skelton, Robin. *Talismanic Magic.* York Beach, Maine: Samuel Weiser, 1985.

Skelton, Robin. *The Practice of Witchcraft Today.* Secaucus, N.J., Citadel Press, 1990.

Smith, Steven. *Wylundt's Book of Incense.* York Beach, Maine: Samuel Weiser, 1989.

Starhawk. *The Spiral Dance*. San Francisco: Harper and Row, 1979.

Valiente, Doreen. *Witchcraft for Tomorrow*. New York: St. Martin's Press, 1978.

About the Author

Lady Sabrina is an initiated priestess of the Wiccan religion and the founder of Our Lady of Enchantment, the largest federally recognized Wiccan seminary in the United States. During the last 20 years, Lady Sabrina has taught more than 25,000 students worldwide how to develop their personal power through Witchcraft and magick. She has appeared on major television shows and is the author of several books, including *Exploring Wicca* (also from New Page Books), *Secrets of Modern Witchcraft Revealed*, and *Reclaiming the Power*. Sabrina lives in New Hampshire with her three dogs, two cats, and assorted fish. She enjoys crafts, gardening, antiquing, and classic horror movies.

For more information about Our Lady of Enchantment or to contact the author, write to:

Our Lady of Enchantment
P.O. Box 1366
Nashua, NH 03061

or visit: www.wiccaseminary.org

ALSO BY LADY SABRINA